An Event-Based Science Module

FIRE!

Student Edition

Russell G. Wright

Needham, Massachusetts
Upper Saddle River, New Jersey

The developers of Event-Based Science have been encouraged and supported at every step in the creative process by the superintendent and board of education of Montgomery County Public Schools, Rockville, Maryland (MCPS). The superintendent and board are committed to the systemic improvement of science instruction, grades preK–12. EBS is one of many projects undertaken to ensure the scientific literacy of all students.

The developers of *Fire!* pay special tribute to the editors, publisher, and reporters of *USA TODAY* and NBC News. Without their cooperation and support, the creation of this module would not have been possible.

Photographs: All Photographs ©Pearson Education/Prentice Hall College unless otherwise noted.
Cover: Jeff Vanuga/Corbis. Student Photographs: Kathy DePalma.
10: Teri Stratford. 3, 5, 24, 30, 44, 45, 71: Courtesy of Mali & Geoffrey Apple. 35: Courtesy of U.S. Department of Agriculture, Forest Service.
Illustrations: 2: Mapping Specialists.

This material is based on work supported by the National Science Foundation under grant number ESI-9550498. Any opinions, findings, conclusions, or recommendations expressed in this publication are those of the Event-Based Science Project and do not necessarily reflect the views of the National Science Foundation.

Copyright © 2005 by the Event-Based Science Institute. Published by Pearson Education, Inc., publishing as Pearson Prentice Hall, Upper Saddle River, NJ 07458. All rights reserved. Printed in the United States of America. This publication is protected by copyright, and permission should be obtained from the publisher prior to any prohibited reproduction, storage in a retrieval system, or transmission in any form or by any means, mechanical, photocopying, recording, or likewise. The publisher hereby grants permission to reproduce pages 72 and 73 for classroom use only, the number not to exceed the number of students in each class. For information regarding permission(s), write to Event-Based Science Institute, Inc., 6609 Paxton Road, Rockville, MD 20850.

Pearson Prentice Hall™ is a trademark of Pearson Education, Inc.
Pearson® is a registered trademark of Pearson plc.
Prentice Hall® is a registered trademark of Pearson Education, Inc.

ISBN: 0-13-166638-X

2 3 4 5 6 7 8 9 10   09 08 07 06

Contents

Project Team	iv
Preface	v
The Story	
Part 1	1
Part 2	12
Part 3	30
Part 4	47
The Task	3
Science Activities	
Oxidation Fixation	8
Blaze Arrest	15
Get Out!	27
A Very Extinguished Career	40
All Fired Up	59
Old Faithful Bounces Back?	63
Discovery Files	
What Is Fire?	10
A Glossary of Fire Terms	14
Oxygen: Who Needs It?	24
Fuel: What Matters to a Fire	26
Fire Myths	32
Put 'em Out or Let 'em Burn?	34
Kindling Point	38
The Ecology of Forest Fires	39
Sprinklers, Smoke Detectors, and Fire Extinguishers	44
Recovery After a Wildfire	46
Food Keeps Your "Fire" Burning	50
Energy 101	53
The Greenhouse Effect	54
Is the Sun on Fire?	58
What's Really Burning?	62
Recent Disasters and Near-Disasters	64
On the Job	
Fire Safety Expert	20
Fire Information Officer	28
Veteran Firefighter	42
Fire Inspector	56
Interdisciplinary Activities	
Social Studies: Calamity Laws	66
Math: Warm-up Activities	67
Math: Slow Down Those Fire Trucks	68
English: Descriptive Writing	70
Performance Assessment	
Writing to Persuade	71
Science Safety Rules	74

Project Team

Author
Russell G. Wright, with a significant contribution from Katarina Stenstedt, and the Montgomery County Public Schools teachers listed under "Science Activities," "Teacher Advisors," and "Interdisciplinary Activities."

Science Activities
*Elaine Chang, Tilden Middle School, Rockville, MD
*Frank S. Weisel, Tilden Middle School, Rockville, MD

Teacher Advisors
*Joyce Bailey, Julius West Middle School, Rockville, MD
*Patricia L. Berard, Colonel E. Brooke Lee Middle School, Silver Spring, MD
*Kathy Devine, Viers Mill Elementary School, Silver Spring, MD
*Barbara Dietsch, T.W. Pyle Middle School, Bethesda, MD
*Emelia Gonzalez, Argyle Middle School, Silver Spring, MD
*William Krayer, Gaithersburg High School, Gaithersburg, MD
*Henry Milne, Cabin John Middle School, Potomac, MD
*Michelle Smetanick, Ridgeview Middle School, Gaithersburg, MD
*Thomas Smith, Briggs Chaney Middle School, Silver Spring, MD
*Kay Stieger, Westland Middle School, Bethesda, MD
*James Sweeney, Kingsview Middle School, Germantown, MD
*Debbie Symons, Cabin John Middle School, Potomac, MD
*Barbara Teichman, Parkland Middle School, Rockville, MD
*Alvanell Thompson, Robert Frost Middle School, Rockville, MD

Interdisciplinary Activities
Lauren Bascom, Grove City College, Grove City, PA
*James J. Deligianis, Tilden Middle School, North Bethesda, MD
*Phyllis Vestal, Gaithersburg Middle School, Gaithersburg, MD

Interns
Susan Buffington, Salisbury State University, Salisbury, MD
Heather McDonald, University of Maryland, College Park, MD
Jessica Phelan, University of Maryland, College Park, MD

Event/Site Support
Kathy DePalma, Bunnell, FL

Scientific Review
Dorothy K. Hall, National Aeronautic and Space Administration
Noel Raufasté, National Institute of Standards and Technology

Student Consultants
*Tilden Middle School, Rockville, MD
Tyler Allard, Patricia Chen, Ryanne Clarke, Nora Desruisseaux, Jeff Hall, Kathleen Leary, Lauren Morse, Tim Pskowski, Thomas Redmond, Louise Wingfield

Field-Test Teachers
Patricia Flynn, Agawam Junior High School, Feeding Hills, MA
Helen Linn, Huron Middle School, Northglenn, CO
George Head, Kirtland Middle School, Kirtland, NM
Terri Lyles and Wendy Reid, Garrett Morgan School of Science, Cleveland, OH
Cheryl Glotfelty and Darren Wilburn, Northern Middle School, Accident, MD
Erin Braben and Cynthia Osborne, Prairieview Middle School, Prairieview, LA
Festus Vanjah and Renekki Wilson, Roper Middle School, Washington, DC
Wendy Beavis and Mike Geil, Tanana Middle School, Fairbanks, AL

EBS Advisory Committee
Joseph Antensen, Baltimore City Public Schools
Deanna Beane, Association of Science-Technology Centers
MaryAnn Brearton, American Association for the Advancement of Science
Jack Cairns, Delaware Department of Public Instruction
Gerard Consuegra, Montgomery County Public Schools
Bob Dubill and Robin Cherry, *USA TODAY*
Gary Heath, Maryland State Department of Education
Henry Heikkinen, University of Northern Colorado
Ramon Lopez, American Physical Society
J. David Lockard, University of Maryland (Emeritus)
Wayne Moyer, Montgomery County Public Schools (Retired)
Arthur Popper, University of Maryland

* Asterisks indicate Montgomery County Schools

Preface

The Event-Based Science Model

Fire! is a module on ecology, chemistry, and energy that follows the Event-Based Science (EBS) instructional model. You will watch videotaped news coverage about wildfires in Yellowstone National Park. You will also read authentic newspaper accounts of other files. Your discussions about fire and the nature of wildfires will show you and your teacher that you already know a lot about the physical-science concepts involved in the event. Next, a real-world task puts you and your classmates in the roles of planners who have been asked to design an outdoor-education camp. The camp you are designing will take the place of one that was just destroyed by a forest fire. You have the responsibility to make the new camp as safe as possible for the children who will use it. You will probably need more information before you begin designing the new camp. If you do, *Fire!* provides hands-on science activities and a variety of readings to give you some of the background you will need. About halfway through the module, you will be ready to begin the task. Your teacher will assign you a role to play and turn you and your team loose to complete the task. You will spend the rest of the time in this module working on that task.

Scientific Literacy

Today, a literate citizen is expected to know more than how to read, write, and do simple arithmetic. Today, literacy includes knowing how to analyze problems, ask critical questions, and explain events. A literate citizen must also be able to apply scientific knowledge and processes to new situations. Event-Based Science allows you to practice these skills by placing the study of science in a meaningful context.

Knowledge cannot be transferred to your mind from the mind of your teacher or from the pages of a textbook. Nor can knowledge occur in isolation from the other things you know about and have experienced in the real world. The Event-Based Science model is based on the idea that the best way to know something is to be actively engaged in it.

Therefore, the Event-Based Science model simulates real-life events and experiences to make your learning more authentic and memorable. First, the event is brought to life through television news coverage. Viewing the news allows you to be there "as it happened," and that is as close as you can get to actually experiencing the event. Second, by simulating the kinds of teamwork and problem solving that occur every day in our workplaces and communities, you will experience the roles that scientific knowledge and teamwork play in the lives of ordinary people. Thus, *Fire!* is built around simulations of real-life events and experiences that dramatically affected people's lives and environments.

In an Event-Based Science classroom, you become the workers; your product is a solution to a real problem; and your teacher is your coach, guide, and advisor. You will be assessed on how you use scientific processes and concepts to solve problems and on the quality of your work.

One of the primary goals of the EBS project is to place the learning of science in a real-world context and to make scientific learning fun. You should not allow yourself to become frustrated.

Student Resources

Fire! is unlike a regular textbook. An Event-Based Science module tells a story about a real event; it has real newspaper articles about the event, and inserts that explain the scientific concepts involved in the event. It also contains science activities for you to conduct in your science class, and interdisciplinary activities that you may do in English, math, social studies, or technology education classes. In addition, an Event-Based Science module gives you and your classmates a real-world task to do. The task is always done by teams of students, with each team member performing a real-life role while completing an important part of the task. The task cannot be completed without you and everyone else on your team doing their parts. The team approach allows you to share your knowledge and strengths. It also helps you learn to work with a team in a real-world situation. Today, most professionals work in teams.

Interviews with people who actually serve in the roles you are playing are scattered throughout the Event-Based Science module. Throughout the module, middle school students tell about their experiences during fires.

Since this module is unlike a regular textbook, you have much more flexibility in using it.

- You may read **The Story** for enjoyment or to find clues that will help you tackle your part of the task.
- You may read selections from the **Discovery File** when you need help understanding something in the story or when you need help with the task.
- You may read all the **On the Job** features because you are curious about what professionals do, or you may read only the interview with the professional who works in the role you've chosen because it may give you ideas that will help you complete the task.
- You may read the **In the News** features because they catch your eye, or as part of your search for information.
- You will probably read all the **Student Voices** features because they are interesting stories told by middle school students like yourself.

Fire! is also unlike regular textbooks in that the collection of resources found in it is not meant to be complete. You must find additional information from other sources, too. Textbooks, encyclopedias, pamphlets, magazine and newspaper articles, videos, films, filmstrips, the Internet, and people in your community are all potential sources of useful information. If you have access to the World Wide Web, you will want to visit the Event-Based Science home page (www.PHSchool.com/EBS), where you will find links to other sites around the world with information and people that will be very helpful to you. It is vital to your preparation as a scientifically literate citizen of the twenty-first century that you get used to finding information on your own.

The shape of a new form of science education is beginning to emerge, and the Event-Based Science Project is leading the way. We hope you enjoy your experience with this module as much as we enjoyed developing it.

—Russell G. Wright, Ed.D.
Project Director and Principal Author

THE STORY—PART 1

The Fires of Yellowstone

In the spring of 1988, nature started them. In the end, it took the help of nature to put them out. But before it was over, more than 800,000 acres were burned in the park itself and another 600,000 in nearby forests. Thousands of firefighters battled the blazes, and millions of gallons of water and chemicals were dropped on the flames.

And Yellowstone's was not the only big fire. By the end of the summer, millions of acres in the West and Alaska had burned.

Television brought scenes of the Yellowstone fires into living rooms across the country. Watching the news, many people figured the park was ruined. But television had not told the whole story.

The Greater Yellowstone Ecosystem is much larger than the park itself. Yellowstone National Park, neighboring Grant Teton National Park, three national wildlife refuges, seven national forests, and private lands in three states make up an ecosystem that covers 28,000 square miles.

Yellowstone National Park, the oldest and first national park in the world, is about the size of Rhode Island and Delaware combined. The park alone covers 3400 square miles, or about 2.2 million acres. Much of it is located in the northwest corner of Wyoming, with areas in Idaho and Montana. It is our only national park with hot springs, geysers, and steam vents. Igneous rock formed more than 600,000 years when volcanic magma cooled to create these natural wonders and tourist attractions.

The Yellowstone fires of 1988 began as many fires do in the forest: with a lightning strike.

Yellowstone Fires of 1988: A Chronology

May Lightning strikes a tree in the northeast part of Yellowstone near Rose Creek; rain extinguishes it later in the day. Park officials assume the rains will put out new fires too. Summers in Yellowstone are short and often rainy.

June 14 A lightning strike starts a fire north of the park in the Storm Creek drainage area in a national forest. U.S. Forest Service officials decide to let it burn.

June 23 A flash of lightning starts a fire in lodgepole trees around Shoshone Lake in the southwest corner of the park. Within a few weeks, eight fires are burning, six caused by lightning. The lightning-caused fires are allowed to burn, but the two caused by human carelessness are fought from the beginning. The different approaches to these different fires are based on the official fire-fighting policy.

June 25 Lightning ignites fires in Targhee National Forest and in the Fan Creek area of northwestern Yellowstone. The Targhee fires are extinguished, but the Fan Creek fire is allowed to burn. Two days later, the Fan Creek fire has spread. Winds whip the fire and, by about a week later, the Fan Creek fire has burned 1800 acres.

July 10 Rain falls and quenches flames in parts of the park. It is the last significant rain that will fall for two months.

Mid July Lightning ignites more fires in the Greater Yellowstone Ecosystem. Warm winds fan the fires. Close to 10,000 acres have already burned. Smoke jumpers (firefighters who parachute to hard-to-reach locations) are sent to put out a human-caused fire near Shoshone Lake. Overhead crews are called in. Park officials start to put firefighters on naturally occurring fires too; the park has abandoned its policy of letting naturally caused forest fires burn. Officials decide that all fires, no matter what the cause, will be fought.

July 22 In the Targhee National Forest near the Yellowstone border in Idaho, a woodcutter drops a cigarette as he leaves the area. Within an hour, a fire is reported to a park ranger. The fire crosses into Yellowstone. Targhee firefighters use bulldozers to build a containment line around the fire. But it's too late—this blaze cannot be contained. It will become known as the North Fork fire.

Winds continue to blow the fires, causing them to grow and spread. Oxygen feeds the flames, which race through the tops, or crowns, of the trees (the canopy). *Snags*—dead trees that are still standing—burn like kindling. The flames move at the incredible rate of 4 to 5 miles per day, sometimes faster.

July 27 A fire threatens Old Faithful Geyser, but it turns south just in time. Some firefighters think the threat from the south is diminishing. They have almost forgotten about the Fan Creek fire still burning in the north.

The greatest fire-fighting effort in U.S. history is now underway. Hundreds of firefighters are sent to battle 8 different fires. By now, more than 50 smaller fires have also been started by lightning. Old fires continue to spread, and smaller ones grow larger. Park officials and firefighters wait for rain.

August 3 Officials meet to plan strategies to control the fires. Six percent of the park (121,000 acres) has already burned. Experts predict the fires will burn no more than 200,000 acres. They predict the fires will begin to slow down. But by August 12, the total area burned exceeds 201,000 acres.

August 19 In the first 10 days of August, new fires ignite and older fires come back to life. Gale-force winds gust to 60 miles per hour. Embers blow downwind from smoldering fires and start new ones.

August 20, "Black Saturday" More than 150,000 acres inside the park and in neighboring forests burn on this one day alone.

Early September Most fires in the park are totally out of control. Fire is again heading for Old Faithful Geyser and the nearby Old Faithful Inn. Both are directly in the fire's path. But at the last minute, the winds shift and the fire turns away.

September 10 Heavy rains begin to fall on the area around Old Faithful Inn.

September 11 Snow arrives. The worst is over. Fires smolder in the park and nearby areas.

November 1988 Heavy snows fall in the Rockies. The fires are out for good.

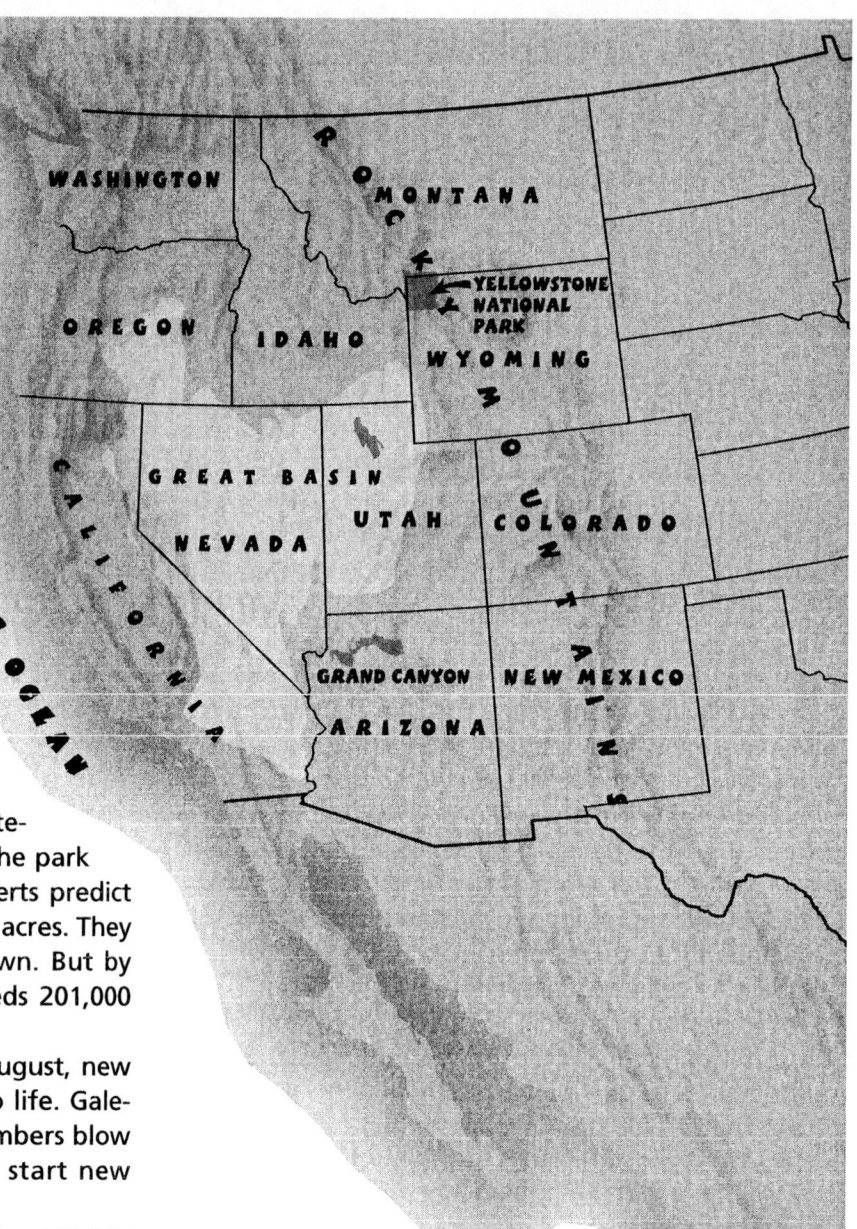

Discussion Questions

1. If you have ever been in a fire, tell what it was like. Describe how it started; how it sounded, smelled, and felt; and, what emotions you experienced.

2. Is the sun on fire? Explain.

3. Name the three ingredients necessary for a fire.

4. What is the best way to put out a fire? Explain why that method works.

5. Are forest fires always bad? Explain.

THE TASK
Rebuilding Muddy Knee

Every year for the past 25 years, sixth graders from Forest County Public Schools have spent seven days at Camp Muddy Knee at the foot of Major Mountain. Their stay has included the study of the interdependence among plants, animals, and the environment. They also learn about camping, outdoor cooking, rock climbing, the natural history of the area, and outdoor safety and survival.

The students have always spent four days living in nice warm cabins before leaving on a three-day backcountry hike that takes them through densely wooded forests and up the steep-sided Major Mountain. From this rugged outdoor experience at Muddy K—that's what the kids call the camp—students developed an appreciation for the outdoors and a love of nature.

But that's all in the past. A month ago today, a forest fire destroyed the buildings and some of the woods and fields surrounding the camp. The strong prevailing wind whipped the fire, causing it to spread rapidly. Luckily, a heavy rain helped firefighters knock down the blaze before it could burn the whole forest.

Fire investigators are still working on the case. So far they haven't ruled out *any* of the possible causes. These are the factors they have determined could have led to the fire:
- For 25 years, no fires had hit the area.
- For two months before the blaze, there was no rain. Trees and underbrush were extremely dry.
- Just before the fire was spotted, a violent thunderstorm moved through the area. The storm brought little rain but very heavy lightning.
- Investigators have uncovered evidence of an electrical short circuit near where the fire began.
- To make matters more confusing, scorched cans labeled "Flammable Liquid" were found in the ruins.

The forest surrounding the buildings suffered heavy losses. No underbrush was left, and few trees survived—those trees still living are charred and may not live very long. Squirrels and other small, ground-dwelling animals fled and have not come back. Some deer were killed, and the ones lucky enough to escape haven't returned either.

School officials, worried that next year's sixth grade class might not have the Muddy Knee experience, hired three consulting firms to come up with plans for rebuilding the camp. All the plans had certain things in common:
- seven bunkhouses (each with two bathrooms and space for 10 double-decker bunk beds)
- one classroom building (contains one laboratory-style classroom, a library, two bathrooms, and an office for the camp director)
- one mess hall with kitchen (space for tables to seat 150)
- one bonfire area
- one covered picnic area

The plans also had major differences. The first firm recommended building a new camp at the same location. The second recommended relocating the camp to a new location, shown on the map on page 4. The third firm recommended moving the camp buildings to a different location based on safety and the needs of the program, but they didn't select a specific place. They're leaving that up to you and the other designers.

The Task 3

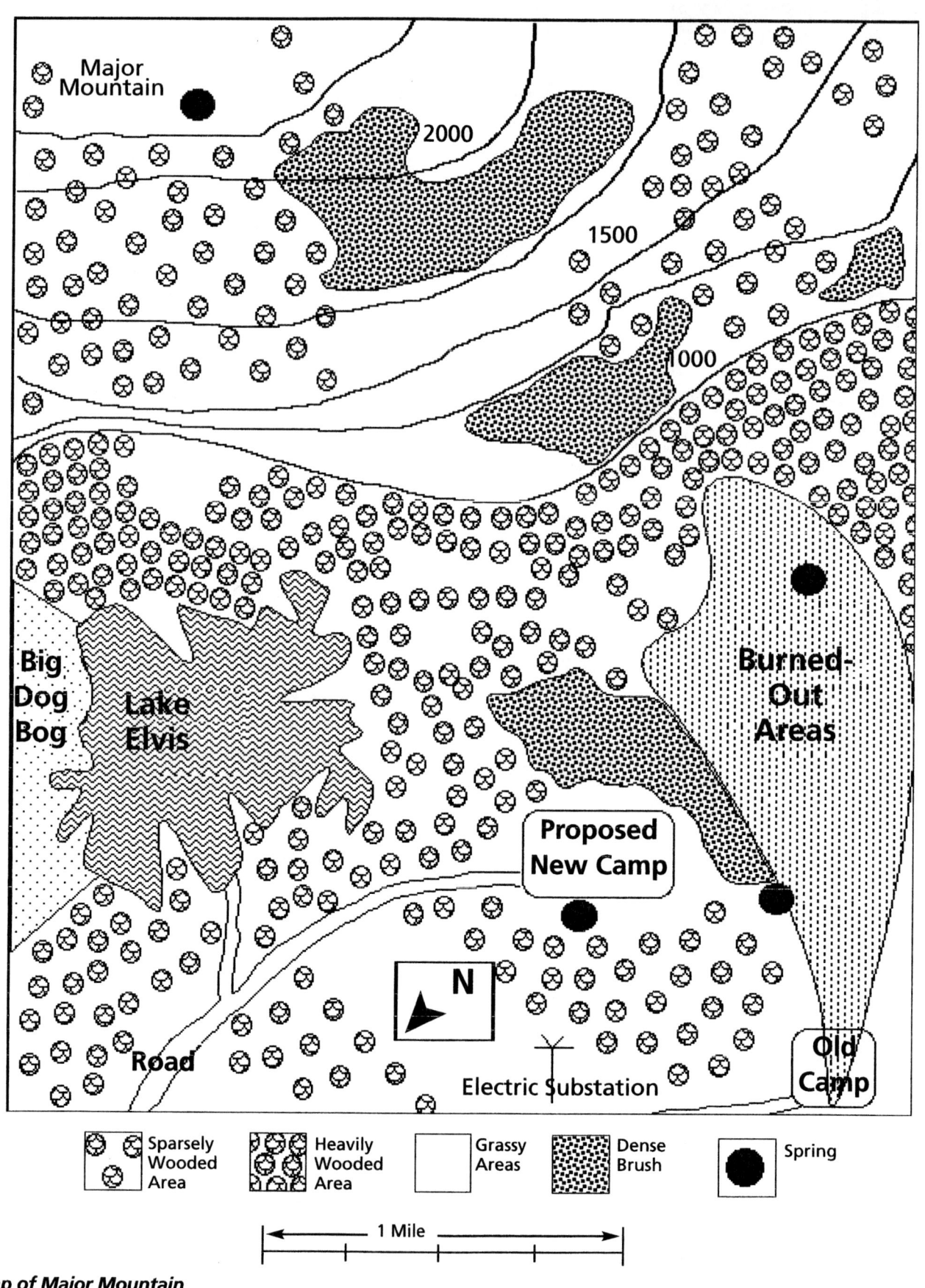

Map of Major Mountain

4   *Fire!*

Designing an Environmental Camp

Now that the consultants have made their recommendations, it's time for you to help choose the location for the new camp buildings. You are an expert on fire and its effects. You have been hired as part of a team of other experts to work with Project BASECAMP (Building Attractive and Safe Environmental Camps Amid Marshes and Phorests).

Your mission is to design a plan for the new facility at Camp Muddy Knee. You will evaluate the recommendations of the consultants using the map on page 4. Then you will design and locate the new buildings for the camp. In five weeks, you must be ready to present and explain your plan at a hearing before the Forest County School Board—or in front of your science class and teacher.

Individual responsibilities are listed for each team role. Even though your jobs are mostly different, be sure to share all of your ideas with the other members of your team.

Fire Investigator

With the other members of your team, analyze the various physical settings of the camp property and select the area where you think the new camp buildings should be built.

- Make a poster that shows or explains how to prevent indoor fires.
- Prepare an evacuation plan for the classroom and mess hall.
- Identify all sources of water.
- Decide how electricity will be used in camp buildings.
- Investigate, and then report to your team on, designing fire-safe buildings (number of and placement of exits, fire escapes, and fire alarms).

Fire Safety Expert

With the other members of your team, analyze the various physical settings of the camp property and select the area where you think the new camp buildings should be built.

- Work with the camp director to prepare a fire safety program (skit or lecture) for students arriving for their stay at the camp.
- Plan and diagram a safe way to get electricity to the buildings.
- Plan the location of five electrical outlets in each bunkhouse.

- Make a list of fire-resistant materials that can be used to construct camp buildings.
- Decide on the placement of emergency exits and signs in buildings and the camp.
- Work with the forest ranger to create a brochure on woodland-fire prevention measures and the camp's burn policy.

Camp Director

With the other members of your team, analyze the various physical settings of the camp property and select the area where you think the new camp buildings should be built.

- Work with the fire safety expert to prepare a fire safety program (skit or lecture) for students arriving for their stay at the camp.
- Analyze the topography of the area (as given to you by the forest ranger) and the role it might play during a fire to help your team select the site.
- Draw a map showing the placement of buildings, trails, and other facilities.
- Develop an evacuation plan for the bunkhouses.
- Select and mark the safest locations for campfires and bonfires.

The Task 5

Forest Ranger

With the other members of your team, analyze the various physical settings of the camp property and select the area where you think the new camp buildings should be built.

- Construct a chart that shows both positive and negative effects of fire on living and nonliving things.
- Work with the fire safety expert to create a brochure on woodland-fire prevention measures and the camp's burn policy.
- Prepare plans for evacuating the camp property.
- Analyze the topography of the area, and share this information with the camp director.
- Design environment-friendly landscaping for the areas around the camp buildings.
- Develop a plan to limit underbrush buildup.

Five weeks from now, your team will present its plans and brochures to the Forest County School Board. Your presentation should include facts about fire and how the new camp buildings will resist fire. Be sure each member of your team has completed all assigned tasks as outlined on pages 5 and 6.

It is hoped these plans will be implemented in time to get Camp Muddy Knee up and running before school starts next September. With your help, Forest County Public Schools should be able to carry this tradition into its twenty-sixth year.

IN THE NEWS

Rain desperately needed: Homes and vehicles are in ashes in Geneva, Fla., Sunday in the wake of a rash of wildfires fueled by tinder-dry conditions and gusting winds.

Gunshot may have sparked Fla. brush fire

By Michelle Kibiger
USA TODAY

A spark from gunfire might be responsible for starting one of several major brush fires that engulfed parts of northeastern and central Florida this weekend, fire officials say.

The flames closed Interstate 95, destroyed about 50 structures and charred nearly 4,000 acres of land.

The largest fire, consuming 1,700 acres, started at a hunting camp in Bunnell, located in Flagler County between St. Augustine and Daytona Beach.

"It was so dry and it was so windy that we just couldn't keep up with it," Roy Longo of Flagler County Emergency Management said.

The initial call came from the hunting camp, causing investigators to suspect the fire might have been caused by a spark from a gunshot, Longo said.

Temperatures in parts of Florida topped the 100-degree mark several days last week. In addition, most of the northeastern part of the state has received less than an inch of rain so far this month, said Michael McAllister of the National Weather Service in Jacksonville.

Several hundred people evacuated across the state. Two people were treated for minor injuries, and several firefighters received treatment for smoke inhalation.

Bunnell residents were allowed back into their homes Sunday to collect personal belongings. A shelter at Bunnell Elementary School housed several area residents Sunday night.

Local businesses offered free food and shelter to displaced families.

Though temperatures eased Sunday, winds gusted from 15 to 20 miles per hour.

"That'll flare up a fire and cause it to possibly ignite some other areas," Longo said.

Investigators estimated the damage in Bunnell at $1.4 million. Damage estimates from the other fires were not available Sunday.

Officials closed a 30-mile stretch of I-95 for 16 hours beginning Saturday. Flames jumped the freeway, and smoke kept the road closed until 7:30 a.m. Sunday.

Other fires burned about 1,200 acres near Geneva, northeast of Orlando, and an additional 1,200 acres in Brevard County, northwest of Cocoa Beach.

About 30 structures were destroyed and 300 residents evacuated in Geneva, but no homes were damaged in the Brevard blaze.

A strong high-pressure system along the Gulf of Mexico is sitting over Florida, keeping thunderstorms from developing. Al Sandrik of the National Weather Service said the hot, dry conditions will end later this month.

"Get one tropical storm in here, and this is forgotten," Sandrik said. "It's not going to take a full-blown hurricane to alleviate our problem."

STUDENT VOICES

There were three major fires in Flagler County. In one, 46 houses burned down. Lawns were scorched, businesses were burned down, and forests were blackened—it looked like a war zone. Now there is some green growing back where the black used to be.

It was confusing when we were evacuated, because I was sleeping and they woke me up. I didn't really know what was going on until my sister came in and said that Flagler County was under a mandatory evacuation. We were evacuated during the Fourth of July, and we didn't get to celebrate as much as we wanted to.

Fires are very unpredictable. If a fire is approaching, take everything that's important to have—like birth certificates, insurance papers, and anything else you will need to help you live just in case you lose your home.

It sounds cliché, but I'd like to say "thank you" to the firefighters.

KATHLEEN GO
PALM COAST, FL

Roaring flames burst from an upper-story window

The charred remains of what was once a bedroom

SCIENCE ACTIVITY

Oxidation Fixation

Purpose
To remove components of the burning process one at a time from a fire and to demonstrate slow oxidation.

Background
You and your team have decided to check out the area where the new camp will be built. The forest ranger thinks it would be a good idea to camp overnight there, so you load a van with gear and head off to the site of Camp Muddy Knee.

The two-hour drive passes quickly. Before you know it, you're there and camp is set up.

It's a beautiful spring evening with a full moon. There is a chill in the air, so a fire is in order.

You're in charge of building the fire. You very carefully pile some small, dry twigs and ignite them with a match. They burn slowly, so you gently blow on them; your breath makes the flame grow bigger. One of your team members decides to help but blows too hard, and the little flame goes out. All that's left is smoke. You have to start all over again. Finally, with no help this time, you get a roaring campfire.

The conversation around the fire is relaxing and, before you know it, the logs are gone and the fire is nothing but red-hot coals. When a team member stumbles in the dark, an empty can is kicked into the coals. It's unanimous; you will leave the can there until morning.

Half your team decide to go to sleep, and half decide to stay up and enjoy the warmth of the glowing coals. An hour and a half later, the coals are scattered, the area is flooded with water, and the fire is covered with soil. There is no doubt: this fire is safely out.

The next morning, it's your job to prepare the fire pit for the breakfast fire. You remove soggy, charred pieces of wood and one rusty can that looks like it was left over from the Civil War.

In this activity, you will compare the chemistry of fire with the chemistry of rusting.

Materials
For each team:

Procedure step 1
- large heatproof jar or beaker
- utility candle
- matches
- goggles
- clay ball about $\frac{1}{2}$ inch in diameter

Procedure step 2
- clear plastic cup
- steel wool

- water
- scissors
- shallow tub or pan
- masking tape

Procedure step 3
- fireproof (not paper) plate
- candle
- matches
- meterstick

Procedure step 4
- metal pan (pie pan or large coffee can)
- sand
- balance
- toothpicks
- tweezers
- match

Procedure
Brainstorm with your team a list of the things that are needed to make a fire burn. Title the list "Fire Components." As you are completing the procedures that follow, you have two jobs:
- Record your observations in a journal.
- Compare your list of fire components with the lists made by the other teams in your class.

Before starting, try to narrow your list to only three things that all fires need to burn. Make a check mark next to fire components you have in common with other teams. Now try to decide which components are absolutely necessary to have a fire, and use the following experiments to test your list. **Caution:** Wear goggles during all controlled burns.

1. Use the small ball of clay to hold a candle upright. Light the candle, and place a jar upside down over it. Make a series of drawings to show what happens from the time you light the candle. Next to each drawing explain, in your own words, the process that is occurring. Compare your explanations with those from other teams.

   Which fire component from your list does this procedure demonstrate? Did you notice substances forming on the inside of the beaker?

   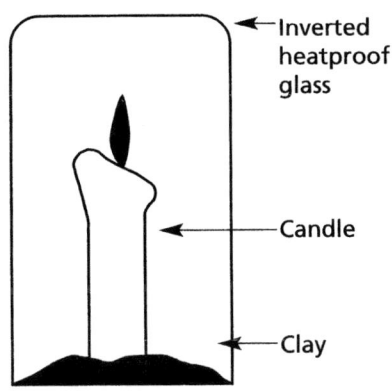

2. Label a clear plastic cup with your names, and turn it upside down. Next, figure out a way to get a wet piece of steel wool to remain in the *bottom* of the upside-down cup and to stay wet. Make certain that the steel wool stays in the bottom of the cup and that the humidity in the cup stays high for a few days. Record daily observations in a journal until a noticeable change occurs.

   One of the components of a fire causes the change you observe. Which fire component from your list does this procedure demonstrate? Explain your answer. (This is a tough one. Don't be frustrated if you can't figure it out. People who get this answer right probably did the experiment before.)

3. Read this part thoroughly, and develop a chart or table in which you will record predictions and results. Put a plate on a table. Stick a candle to the plate using a bit of melted wax, and light it. From a safe distance, blow the candle out. Light and blow out the candle several more times, each time moving farther away. Stop moving back when you can no longer blow out the candle. Record all distances in your journal.

   Which fire component does this procedure demonstrate?

4. Pour a layer of sand into a metal container. Determine the mass of one toothpick (if your balance isn't sensitive enough to weigh just one toothpick, weigh more than one and divide to get an average). Stand one toothpick up in the sand. Hold another toothpick with tweezers, and with a match, light the end of this toothpick. Use the burning toothpick to light the base of the toothpick in the sand, just above the level of the sand. Observe the experiment until there is no more reaction. Remove the burned toothpick from the sand, and determine its mass again. In your journal, record your observations and measurements.

   Which fire component does this procedure demonstrate?

   Review your journal notes and compare them with other teams' notes.

Conclusion

The producers of *Rosemary Road*, a local children's TV show, have designated the letter *F* and the number 3 as today's "sponsors." One of the *F* words they have chosen to feature is *Fire*. They want your team of fire experts to make a 20-second skit about one of the components of a fire. Review your notes, and write an informative presentation on one of the three fire components that you have explored. Be sure little kids will understand the point you are trying to make.

Present your infomercial to the class.

The Story—Part 1

DISCOVERY FILE

What Is Fire?

Fire is a chemical reaction. Technically speaking, fire refers to the heat, light, and smoke produced by burning materials.

The Fire Triangle
A fire requires three things to burn:
- oxygen
- fuel
- heat

This is the fire triangle. Take away one of the sides of the triangle, and the fire goes out.

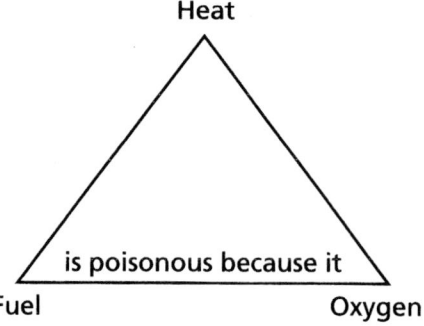

Oxygen
Oxygen feeds a fire. A fire will not burn without oxygen because fire, as defined, is the rapid chemical reaction between a fuel and oxygen. It may seem a paradox that the invisible gas essential to our survival is also essential to fire, which can kill us. But this is because the process by which our bodies use oxygen to release energy from food (*respiration*) is very similar to the process of fire, only slower.

Oxygen itself does not burn; it simply reacts with the fuel. You probably know that fires need oxygen because you have heard that fires can be *smothered* to put them out. Smothering a fire means covering it so that oxygen cannot get to the fuel.

You also know that fires burn better when extra oxygen is added—that is what happens when you blow on a fire to get it going, or when the wind causes a forest fire to burn faster and hotter.

During a fire, fuel combines with oxygen to form CO_2 (carbon dioxide) and water. Large amounts of heat energy, as well as light energy, are released. When there isn't quite enough oxygen present, *incomplete combustion* occurs. In this kind of burning, which happens inside automobile engines, a deadly gas known as carbon monoxide (CO) is released. Carbon monoxide is poisonous because it binds tightly with *hemoglobin* in the blood and prevents blood from carrying oxygen.

A few centuries ago, people thought an invisible substance they called "phlogiston" was present in flammable materials. Phlogiston was said to be without color, taste, odor, or weight, and to be given off during burning. The ash of a burned material was believed to be the true material with its phlogiston removed. That theory was discarded in 1774, after Antoine Lavoisier, a French chemist, discovered the role of oxygen in combustion and gave oxygen its name.

Fuel
Fuel is any substance that will combine rapidly with oxygen to produce heat and light. What makes a good fuel?

Wood and paper are good fuels; water is not. Fuels come in many forms: solid, liquid, and gas. But most fuels are large molecules made of carbon combined with hydrogen and sometimes other elements. These large molecules have energy from the sun stored in them. When fuel burns, oxygen reacts with it to break it down into smaller compounds—usually carbon dioxide and water. This process releases the energy that was holding the molecules together.

Liquid fuel—specifically gasoline, which comes from petroleum—is what your car runs on. Your house or apartment may be heated by a solid fuel like coal or wood, but more likely it is heated by a gaseous fuel called natural gas.

When anything burns, it's not the solid or liquid that actually burns—it's the vapors or gas that come from the fuel when it becomes so hot that it vaporizes.

10   *Fire!*

Heat

Heat is necessary for a fire, because a fuel must be heated until it reaches its *ignition temperature*—the lowest temperature at which the fuel will burn. Every material has its own ignition temperature, or kindling point. (See the Discovery File "Kindling Point" on page 38.)

A fire usually starts with materials that ignite easily. As the fire grows, it radiates more heat, causing the fire to grow more rapidly. Eventually, an enclosed fire—like a fire in a room—reaches what is called *flashover*. At this point, all materials in the room reach their ignition temperatures and anything that is not yet on fire bursts into flames. At flashover, the room itself is full of fire. Flashover cannot be survived for more than a second or two, even with the best fire-rated suits and helmets. If a room is about to reach flashover, firefighters get out fast.

No material can be completely fireproof. Chemicals can be added to make materials fire resistant by raising their ignition temperatures, but even fire-retardant materials will eventually burn.

Controlling Fire

Firefighters refer to a "fire tetrahedron"—the three essential components from the fire triangle, plus a fourth: the chain reaction that happens as the fire burns and spreads "like wildfire."

The only way to suppress—knock down or put out—a fire is by removing one of the three components. Basically, this is what a fire extinguisher does, cooling the fire to remove the heat or smothering it to remove oxygen.

Wildfires typically burn 5 million acres in the United States annually, costing hundreds of millions of dollars. And the price tag can only grow larger as urban sprawl encroaches on forests nationwide, say experts. Large, violent wildfires can generate their own controlling weather. The released heat can spawn deep convection, even thunderstorms, with strong and dangerous winds. So-called *fire whirls*, cousins of tornadoes, hurl flaming logs and other burning debris to locations miles away, setting other areas ablaze.

Fires can be controlled to some extent by regulating the amount of available fuel and oxygen. However, a forest fire that is fed by gusting winds and has an almost unending supply of fuel will quickly become uncontrollable.

STUDENT VOICES

The wind just started blowing, and the fires just kept on jumping from one spot to another. It was scary and frightening because I didn't know what to do. I was afraid my house would burn down and we would have nothing left. My house just melted on the side, and the businesses had smoke damage.

During the fires, my grandmother was transferred from one nursing home to another, but she couldn't take it anymore. She passed away during the fires.

Now the grass has started turning green, and the trees and flowers have started coming up again.

TONIANN DURANTE
PALM COAST, FL

The Story—Part 2
Aftermath and Legacy

Ten years after the fires swept through Yellowstone National Park and much of the Greater Yellowstone Ecosystem, nature was once again working its magic: renewal was well underway. After all, fire has been a natural part of this region since it was formed.

Fire shaped the land thousands of years before humans arrived and long before recorded history. The fires of '88 were dramatic in their devastation—bringing about noticeable changes to wilderness areas—but in the larger scheme of things, they were but a blip on the geologic time scale. And as devastating as the fires seemed, they were beneficial in many ways. It made a good story at the time, but the fires were not the catastrophe they seemed to be.

The Benefits of Forest Fires

The popular view of forest fires is that they are bad for the forest. But nature and science tell us otherwise. Much of Earth's plant and animal life depends on fire for its survival. Many species thrive on fire.

The eight huge fires that burned during the summer of 1988 in and around Yellowstone were made much worse by two factors: one, an extreme drought that summer; and two, the *lack* of recent fires in the area. Looking back, many forest ecologists remarked that the fires of 1988 were long overdue.

Because of the park's burn policy, in place since 1972, many forest fires that should have been allowed to burn were *knocked down*. This policy meant that over a period of many decades, an enormous *fuel load* of dead wood and leaves was building up on the forest floor, making the Yellowstone forests much more susceptible to an even larger wildfire.

One of the benefits of periodic fires in a forest is that they keep the fuel load down. This prevents *kindling* from accumulating throughout the forest.

Fire ecologists—scientists who study how people, plants, and animals live with fire—have learned that forest fires promote *biodiversity*, or biological diversity among the numbers of different plant and animal species in an environment.

In what other ways does a forest benefit from wildfire?

- Fire burns off decaying material such as fallen logs and limbs that have collected on the forest floor.
- Burned material adds nutrients to the soil.
- Enriched soil encourages new growth of plant species.
- New plant species that spring up after a devastating fire attract new animal species to the region.
- Fire can thin out the canopy at the top of the forest. Without a fire, the canopy can become so dense that sunlight doesn't penetrate to the newer, younger growth on the forest floor.
- Some species of plants are dependent on fire for their regrowth. These *fire species*, as they are called, have unique adaptations for surviving and regenerating in fire. Here are some examples:

Lodgepole pines, which produce two types of cones: the first kind opens at maturity,

12   Fire!

but the second opens only when heated. Yellowstone's forests are about 80% lodgepole pines, so nature has evolved a way for the trees to reseed themselves after a fire. Squirrels and other small mammals eat the seeds released from the cones, further spreading them.

Ponderosa pine is another fire species in the American West. Like the lodgepole pine, the seeds of this pine are surrounded by a resin that must melt before seeds can be released.

Chaparral, a shrub that grows in the West, also contains seeds that open when exposed to intense heat. The chaparral itself becomes fuel for the wildfire that is necessary for the plant to reproduce itself.

Fireweed, aptly named, springs up quickly after a forest fire. These pink-flowered plants rapidly spread over newly burned ground in the spring following the Yellowstone fires.

Aspen lose their leaves and buds in a fire. But their underground root systems quickly produce many young shoots after a fire.

Douglas fir has adapted to fire by its self-pruning ability. They do not have lower branches, so a fire does not have a "ladder" to climb. Older firs have thick bark to protect them from fire.

After the fires of 1988, the Yellowstone area experienced all the beneficial consequences of the same fire that many people feared would permanently damage the park. By the fall of 1988, many lodgepole-pine seeds covered the forest floor. Wildflower seedlings could be seen by the spring and summer of 1989, and less than two years after the fires, Yellowstone National Park enjoyed a bumper crop of wildflowers that grew up through the ashes to bloom.

Most of the park's animals were fine. Contrary to myth and movies, animals do not flee a forest fire in a pack, the way the deer did in *Bambi.* Many of the animals survive better than people do in a wildfire. Those that die usually are overcome by smoke. Fire is nature's way of thinning out older and weaker animals.

The park also had an increase in tourism in the fall of 1988 and in years to follow, putting to rest another fear.

Now a new generation of lodgepole pines is growing—even in the most burned areas of the park. Trout, birds, and large mammals are also doing well, thanks to the lush new growth that resulted from the fire.

Park ecologist Don Despain often takes visiting reporters and other scientists on a tour of the park to show them just how the wilderness has renewed itself. Because the burn patterns occurred in what is called a *mosaic* (varying degrees of intensity), biodiversity was encouraged even more by the fires of 1988.

The National Center for Supercomputing Applications developed a computer simulation to model what the Yellowstone region would have looked like *without* any fires from 1690 to the present time. Their model showed a region with very little diversity and much less food for ground-feeding animals. It seems that the entire web of life is positively affected by fire.

Yellowstone National Park and the Greater Yellowstone Ecosystem have been and continue to be a giant laboratory-in-the-wilderness for learning about the role fire plays in the ecosystem.

DISCOVERY FILE

A Glossary of Fire Terms

Combustion The burning of a gas, liquid, or solid in which the fuel is rapidly oxidized, or consumed, producing heat and usually light.

Firebreak A strip of plowed or cleared land created to stop a forest or prairie fire from spreading.

Firestorm A large forest fire with a column of air rising so rapidly above it that the fire itself draws strong winds into its base. A firestorm may be accompanied by rain. *Firestorm* can also refer to a fire that is raging out of control, such as one caused by oil or gas.

Firewall A partition built to keep fire from spreading from one part of a building or ship to another.

Flashover The moment when a fire becomes so hot that every flammable object in the area is emitting gases that burst into flame. The most sophisticated gear cannot keep a firefighter safe when the temperature reaches this point. If they see vapors rising from an upholstered couch, firefighters know that a flashover is imminent. If firefighters stay in the flashover, their suits are likely to melt on their bodies. A flashover can reach a temperature of 1200°F.

Flash point The lowest temperature at which enough vapors are given off by liquid that it will ignite when a flame is applied. Hazardous chemicals have low flash points. Flash points of three common substances are propane, –156°F (–104°C); ethyl ether, –49°F (–45°C); and benzene, 12°F (–11°C).

Kindling temperature, kindling point, or *ignition temperature* The lowest point at which a material will ignite. At this temperature, a chemical reaction called *oxidation* takes place between the material being heated and oxygen in the air.

Spontaneous combustion Burning that begins without heat from an external source. Materials like oily or paint-filled rags stored in the basement seem to suddenly burst into flames. Spontaneous combustion happens when a material reaches its kindling point and self-ignites. Even wet hay can become hot enough from the decaying action of microorganisms to catch fire without the application of a flame.

Note: Some fire-related terms have taken on other meanings. For example, computer programmers create *firewalls* to keep out hackers; a *firestorm* can refer to an intense response.

Searing flames consume a porch

14   *Fire!*

SCIENCE ACTIVITY

Blaze Arrest

Purpose
To invent a fire-retardant material.

Background
As you and your team prepare the plans for new buildings at Camp Muddy Knee, you begin to think of all the things that must go into them. You make a list of the necessary furnishings and notice that most, if not all, are made of materials that are potentially flammable. Seat covers, drapes, mattress covers, pillows, and the like can burn if they are exposed to flames. You've got to find a way to reduce the hazard.

You decide to begin by studying the methods used to make children's sleepwear fire resistant. You have already found an experiment you think might help.

Materials
For each pair:
- 2 swatches each of 4 or 5 types of cloth (cotton, wool, polyester, felt, and so on)
- scissors
- water
- borax
- container, such as a 2-liter soda bottle with the top cut off
- candle
- matches
- goggles
- washtub, bucket, or sink

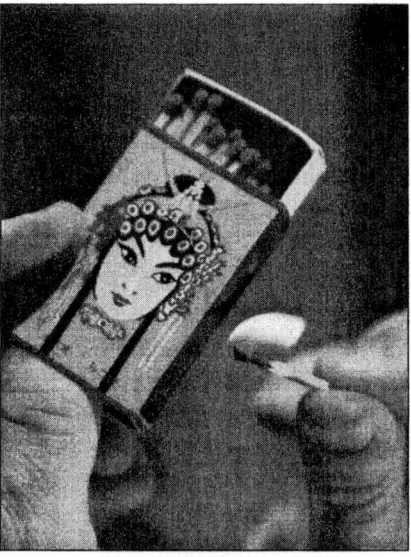

- tongs
- stopwatch
- paper towels

Procedure
Cut each piece of cloth into two smaller pieces. Label each different kind of material. Dissolve a few teaspoons of borax in a liter of water.

Design a fair test to see whether cloth treated with borax is more or less flammable than untreated cloth. You may have to let the treated pieces of cloth dry overnight before they are dry enough to burn. **Caution:** Wear goggles during all controlled burns.

Read the next paragraph, and then set up a data table into which you can record your observations.

Light the candle, and stick it to the bottom of the sink with a drop of hot wax. Use this burning candle and the tongs to conduct your tests. Always hold the tongs at arm's length. Record your observations.

Conclusion
Report your findings in the form of a magazine article to be submitted to *Li'l Tyke's Fire Safety Magazine*. Subscribers to this magazine are manufacturers of toys and clothes designed for children between two and five years old. Your article should explain what you learned about fabric flammability and flame-retardant fabrics. It should include a step-by-step procedure for duplicating your experiment.

Editors of the magazine want you to provide labeled drawings of your experimental setup.

IN THE NEWS

Yellowstone on the mend

Park flourishes a decade after fires

By Chad Stevens, AP; inset by National Park Service

Nature's course: A single flower graces a hillside that was burned when wildfires raged across Yellowstone Park in 1988. The inset photo shows one of those blazes racing through a stand of trees.

Continued on page 17

16   *Fire!*

IN THE NEWS

Scientists and visitors find rapid recovery remarkable

By Patrick O'Driscoll
USA TODAY

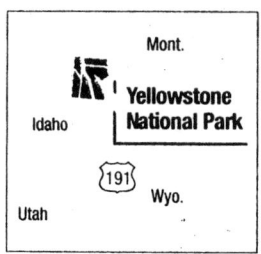

YELLOWSTONE NATIONAL PARK — Down on his knees, nose in the dirt, park biologist Roy Renkin squints at the future through a pocket magnifying glass.

"Yeah, that's a seedling," Renkin announces, standing up again in a thicket of lodgepole pines the size of Christmas trees. "This is really cool."

The two-inch sprig is a lodgepole, too. But this one is a surprise: A second-generation grandchild of the 1988 wildfires that scorched 1,240 square miles of the world's first national park.

The sprout's parent, a 6-foot sapling born in the months after the summer inferno, wasn't supposed to reproduce for another decade or two. But the fires of '88 opened the forest canopy to abundant sunlight and enriched the soil with nutrients from dead trees. Now the branches of the robust sapling bristle with seed cones.

Across Yellowstone National Park, tens of millions of trees have sprung from the ashes of what America and the world assumed was an ecological disaster. A decade after walls of flame roared through more than one-third of the park's 2.2 million acres, Yellowstone's rebirth, swift and vigorous, continues to impress scientists and amaze near-record throngs of tourists.

Yellowstone today is a gigantic laboratory of scientific study and public education about the beneficial effects of wildfire on the land and its inhabitants. Park officials even are studying whether to set controlled burns to clear out more deadwood and other volatile "fuel" in areas missed by the 1988 blazes. Intentionally lighting such "prescribed" fires inside the park would be a Yellowstone first.

USA TODAY, 25 AUGUST 1998

Tree trunks rise in a sunlit forest

IN THE NEWS

Ancient trees need a little help from a friend: Fire

By John Ritter
USA TODAY

SEQUOIA NATIONAL PARK, Calif. — No plant on Earth inspires more awe than giant sequoias, those cathedrals of antiquity that remind humans of their brevity.

Now, proof that wisdom comes with age, the big trees are playing a central role in the evolution of policies on forest fires in public lands.

It was the giant sequoias, some more than 2,500 years old, that taught foresters to revise their thinking about their worst enemy: fire. Today, foresters say they can use sequoias to teach a dubious public that fire is good for a forest.

And none too soon, scientists say. Decades of putting out — or trying to put out — virtually every fire have turned forests into dangerously overgrown tinderboxes, ripe for catastrophe far beyond the 200,000-plus acres burning this week in seven Western states.

By Teresa Hurteau for USA TODAY
Secret to life: Heat opens cones and frees seeds.

The U.S. Forest Service estimates that 39 million acres in national forests alone are at high risk of major wildfires. Setting intentional fires to thin them out, called controlled burning, is a key strategy to ease the danger.

Yet despite a major federal policy shift in 1995, and quadrupled spending since then, the amount of controlled burning in the West remains small. Many forests are so thick with brush and trees that they need to be thinned first with chainsaws, but not nearly enough of that is being done, a General Accounting Office study in April found.

Moreover, an entrenched fire-suppression ethic dies hard, particularly in the face of a misinformed public, outright opposition and clean-air and water mandates.

"We have this vast backlog of literally hun-

Continued on page 19

IN THE NEWS

Sequoias' size, age don't stand alone

Sometimes hailed as the oldest and largest living things, giant sequoias are neither.

Bristlecone pines that inhabit desolate mountaintops in the Great Basin of eastern California and Nevada live at least 5,300 years, compared with 3,200 years for the oldest known sequoia. Alerce trees in Chile and Argentina also live longer.

Aspen groves in the Rockies of Colorado and Utah are clonal; the trees all come from a single individual through root sproutings. Aspen groves can go on for miles with an interrelated root mat; the same apparently is true of the enormous root mats of some forest fungi.

"We've gotten more cautious. We say sequoias are the world's oldest living trees," says Bill Tweed, chief naturalist at Sequoia and Kings Canyon national parks.

Sequoias are in the same family as California coastal redwoods but don't grow as tall. Redwoods reach heights of 367 feet, compared with 311 feet for the tallest sequoia. But sequoias are heftier, up to 40 feet in diameter at their base, compared with 22 feet for redwoods.

Sequoias grow naturally only on the western slope of the Sierra Nevada, between 5,000 feet and 7,000 feet, because of the favorable climate: 40 to 50 inches of annual precipitation, the absence of below-zero temperatures and periodic disturbance from fire. — By John Ritter

IN THE NEWS

Sequoias are reversing thinking on forest fires

dreds of millions of acres throughout the West that are more dangerous now than before fire suppression," Interior Secretary Bruce Babbitt says.

The GAO study predicted a 10-to-25-year window to thin forests "before damage from uncontrollable wildfires becomes widespread." But public opinion and a century-old "10 a.m. policy"— put out fires by 10 the morning after they're discovered — don't change easily. That's where giant sequoias come in. The trees are so revered — three of the first four national parks had them — and they elicit such an emotional reflex in people that they're seen as potentially powerful tools to educate the public about fire.

By using fire to help manage giant sequoia groves in the western Sierra Nevada, the only place on Earth where they grow naturally, foresters believe the public will not only see the value of controlled burning but also be willing to compromise on environmental concerns.

COVER STORY

And cutting the risk of giant conflagrations that threaten lives and property has become an urgent public safety issue throughout the West as urban development nudges up against forests.

"We're strongly supportive of efforts to restore fire to its natural, ecological role," says Jay Watson, Wilderness Society regional director for California and Nevada. "But it's still largely misunderstood by the general public. The public sees smoke in the air and thinks it's a bad thing."

But to a giant sequoia, among the biggest and oldest living things, fire is critical to perpetuating the species. Fire creates openings in the forest canopy that allow sun-loving seedlings to thrive.

With fires suppressed during most of the century, sequoias simply didn't reproduce, except in a few places where logging had cleared openings. Practically no new seedlings took root. That alarming observation, that an entire generation of sequoia reproduction had been lost, sparked a research frenzy. The result was a 30-year learning curve that reshaped fire policy.

By the mid-1960s, scientists knew that the trees needed fire, but when they set off controlled burns in sequoia groves, no seedlings came up. It took a 1977 burn that got out of hand in Kings Canyon National Park to show them why.

A high-intensity fire scorched a 2-acre section, creating a "hot spot" within the much larger controlled blaze. Seedlings sprouted soon after, and scientists saw that low-intensity fire alone wasn't enough. There had to be spots, at least a quarter-acre, where all the other species that competed for water were burned off, where the soil was disturbed and where the heat opened sequoia cones so seeds could fall to the ground.

That had been nature's way, producing a Swiss-cheese mosaic in the 75 known sequoia groves up and down the Sierra. The trees are often found in clusters, three or four or more together, forged out of age-old hot spots.

Nathan Stevenson, a U.S. Geological Survey ecologist, took hundreds of core samples from giant sequoias to show the utter failure of 20th century reproduction. "Fire suppression has had a greater effect on giant sequoias than anything else humans have done," he says.

Scientists also noticed that after years of fire suppression, a lightning-ignited natural wildfire would burn so hot from accumulated brush that it killed mature sequoias. A 250-foot-tall, 20-foot-diameter sequoia is normally resistant to fire. Fire scars it — creating those blackened, hollowed-out "cat faces" around the trunk — but the tree heals and actually grows faster for a while after fires.

Tree rings as time capsules

Core sampling and the study of sequoia tree rings led to discoveries about the history of fire in the Sierras that scientists say have major implications for the 21st century. The rings are remarkable time capsules of year-by-year data on fires and climate.

Some of what was learned seemed self-evident: Fire was more frequent and severe in drier, hotter years and less frequent in wetter years. A pattern became apparent: Fire came often to sequoia forests, every eight to 20 years, and usually at low intensity. Occasionally a severe blaze would rip through.

Samples from groves up and down the Sierra revealed years, as many as five a century, when fire didn't just burn single groves but was prevalent throughout the mountains. Of course, in these "regional" fire years of the past, the forests weren't overgrown as they are today. Today, a regional fire year means millions of dollars in firefighting costs.

Even more sobering was what the rings told scientists about drought. The bottom line: The 20th century has been mild, just four severe droughts compared with as many as 12 in some centuries. Periods of extreme drought were more frequent in the past and "might relate to other aspects of climate," says Malcolm Hughes, director of the Laboratory of Tree-ring Research at the University of Arizona. "But for now we don't know."

Hughes is studying the rings from sequoias and other long-lived Western trees, trying to pinpoint the millennium's worst droughts, those that parched the Southwest and all of California.

"If the river systems in those regions go low for a long time, we've all got a problem," he says. "We want to see what makes that happen, and whether we can forecast it."

So reliable are tree-ring findings — they've been corroborated by other historical and ecological records — that sequoia research is now under the umbrella of national global-change research.

The trees themselves are susceptible to global effects. Mature sequoias appear to be more resistant to ozone pollution than other species, though seedlings aren't. Scott Anderson, an environmental scientist at Northern Arizona University, analyzed the pollen content of ancient soil around sequoia groves and found the trees were far rarer, possibly on the brink of extinction, during a warm period between 11,500 and 5,200 years ago.

If the globe is warming now, as many scientists think, sequoias could be in trouble. And that's a scary thought for forest managers. As much as they appreciate the sequoias' contributions to larger science, they want to know what's best for the trees today.

And what's best seems to be mimicking nature and reintroducing fire to the groves. The problem is, they aren't all uniformly ready for fire. In Sequoia and Kings Canyon national parks, fire has been a tool since the 1960s. Brush and dead vegetation — the fuel load, as foresters call it — is under control, and sequoia regeneration is dramatic.

Today, the hot spot from the '77 fire is thick with young trees, some 40 or 50 feet tall. A few will reach maturity in 150 to 200 years.

But less than half the sequoias are in those two parks and Yosemite. Most are on U.S. Forest Service land, a few on Bureau of Land Management (BLM) land and in state forests. The National Park Service's controlled-burn program is years ahead of other agencies'. Many of their forests may be too overgrown to introduce fire, but to propose thinning with saws arouses suspicion from logging opponents.

The Forest Service and BLM are still trying to get a handle on what they have. They won't finish an inventory and satellite mapping of their groves before next year. Incredibly, new groves are still being discovered. BLM ecologist Russ Lewis found a small, previously unrecorded one this year on Case Mountain, just outside Sequoia.

The Park Service is justifiably proud of its groves, but they are essentially tourist groves.

Every summer, hundreds of thousands of visitors troop up to see the General Sherman tree, the world's biggest. Fewer hike outlying trails to see less-accessible groves.

But on Case Mountain, the groves are wild. Public access is by foot only. There are no hiking trials, no public facilities of any kind. There are giant sequoias that few modern humans have ever seen. The BLM has turned the 23,000-acre mountain over to research, and hydrologists and ecologists are having a field day. But Case is in peril.

Because of fire suppression, brush is so thick in the canyons lacing the mountain that

By Genevieve Lynn, USA TODAY

lightning could ignite a fire hot enough to race up into the groves and kill a lot of 1,000- and 2,000-year-old sequoias.

"It's scary, the density up here," says Ron Fellows, BLM's Bakersfield District field manager. "The place is just ripe. You've got to start applying some fire."

Changing public attitudes

That's at least two or three years away, but Fellows knows how sensitive the subject is to the 3,000 residents of the nearby town of Three Rivers. In a survey last year, 64% of respondents said they'd had smoke-related discomfort from fires. Just 52% agreed that the Park Service should ignite controlled fires and let natural fires burn.

The BLM, the Forest Service, the Park Service and other agencies have formed the Giant Sequoia Ecology Cooperative, one of whose aims is to preach the value of fire. In the marketing campaigns to come, forester managers don't want to retire Smokey Bear so much as have him lean against a giant sequoia. They still want people to be careful not to start forest fires but also to understand that they're necessary sometimes.

Bruce Babbitt likes to point out that a sequoia cone emblem decorates the hatband of park rangers. "We need a symbol for prescribed fire, and this might be the one," he says. "It all began with the sequoias."

By Teresa Hurteau for USA TODAY

Trees 'only' 20 years old: Nathan Stevenson of the U.S. Geological Survey with young sequoias thriving in a break in the forest canopy in Kings Canyon National Park, Calif.

USA TODAY, 2 SEPTEMBER 1999

The Story—Part 2   19

ON THE JOB

Fire Safety Expert

STEVEN KENNEDY
PALO ALTO, CALIFORNIA

Steven Kennedy has fought wildfires in California and produces video about fire safety and environmental issues. More about his work and a fire quiz are available at www2.best.com/~canonbal.

My most memorable science teacher was Mr. Paul Hoag, my biology teacher at Taylor Intermediate School in Millbrae, California. We often sat through a botanical slide show of 100 photos of native California plants . . . like sticky monkey flower, ceanothus, and white oak. I memorized them all.

At the same time, I often went to a friend's cabin in the woods 100 miles north of San Francisco. These 20 acres of land had been logged in the '50s when cut-and-run was in vogue. Lots of good timber was left on the ground, and nothing was done to replant the forest. The land grew back so thick with fir trees and brush that you couldn't walk through it. If you cut a 4-inch-thick fir off at the base, it couldn't fall over. You had to cut it again higher up and pull it down through the tree canopy. And then, if you cut it one more time, maybe you could drag it off to the burn pile.

Hard work like that was heady stuff to a kid like me. And that is why becoming a firefighter was a natural step. My

first firefighter job took me back to the Bay Area in August of '77 to put out the massive fire on Mt. Diablo. I was mighty impressed seeing 40-foot flames wash up the side of that mountain.

At the time of the massive Oakland-Berkeley hills fire in 1991, I was hiking with the Sierra Club and couldn't help but notice how thick the brush was. It wasn't until I got home and turned on the TV that I found out how bad the fire was. Later, when I read an article about the vegetation-management plan proposed for the Mt. Tamalpais watershed, I began to get the idea for a new video project.

Questions about fire safety that you must answer before building a camp fall into three general areas: proper treatment of the land before building; care in the selection of building materials; and a centralized, gravity-fed, fail-safe water supply available year-round for fighting a fire.

A good place to start would be with a vegetation-management plan, or VMP. Determine the current condition of the vegetation and decide what is likely to exist in the future. Your goal is to find ways to reduce *fuel loads* enough to keep fire out of the tree canopy no matter where a fire starts. Your camp-construction team will have to answer a series of questions, including:

- Is this an old-growth, second-growth, or third-growth forest? (Second- and third-growth forests are trees that grow after a forest has been cut down.) Are suitable building materials available on the site, and would it be noticed if they were used up?

- How many tons of fuel per acre are on the property?

- When was the last fire in the area, and what visible damage to the trees remains?

- If the fire safety expert and forest ranger on your team choose to have controlled burns to reduce fuel loads, what percent mortality should be expected among the non-fire-adapted species?

- What pretreatment of the land is necessary before conducting a controlled burn—climbing trees to remove the fuel ladder, or cutting down snags to reduce risks of falling branches and showers of sparks?

- What must be the temperature, relative humidity, and fuel moisture levels in order to ensure a safe burn? Where will the burn hit existing barriers to fire, such as roads, creek beds, and rail lines?

- In which direction will the smoke from a controlled burn drift, and will neighbors complain?

- Will smoke affect traffic on nearby highways?

- What are the soil types underlying the site, and are they highly erodable soils?

- What is the topography of the site? What is the grade of the steepest slopes to be control burned?

Given the assignment of creating something aesthetically pleasing and durable, your camp-construction team would have to ask questions about building materials, including:

- What is the projected overnight sleeping capacity of the camp?

- Can the available sunshine be used to reduce heating costs?

- Can some trees be removed to improve views or create opportunities for solar heating? Are there trees or limbs that should be removed for safety reasons? Can the timber be milled on-site?

- Can rustic, hand-hewn log cabins be built? Should the job go to a general contractor? Is there enough heartwood for the foundations?

- How can sleeping cabins be designed to blend into the landscape? Should the cabins be portable or fixed?

- Should the cabins have sprinkler systems and fire detectors?

- Should the cabins have electricity, indoor toilets, and running water?

- Should the cabins have wood stoves, electric heat, gas heat, or no heat at all? (Remember the lengths to which people will go to stay warm and the dangers of carbon monoxide poisoning and accidental fires.)

- Must the cabins be identical, or can they be custom crafted? (Consider the benefits of mass production versus use of secondhand and recycled building materials, group bonding, handicapped access, ceiling height and heating, and the availability of level ground.)

- What kind of roof should be used? If you choose wood shingles, should they be pressure treated to reduce flammability? If you select a manufactured material, should it be fiberglass shingles that look like wood? Or copper that will quickly turn green? Should the roofs be made of concrete and covered with enough dirt to grow grass? Or should the cabins be dome shaped and have only walls and skylights?

- Should the cabin walls be made of rammed earth, hay bales, or adobe?

- Should we build tree forts with safety nets beneath and live like Ewoks?

Given the likelihood that a rompin' stompin' forest fire will scorch the neighborhood sometime during the next 40 years—despite what the local fire departments can do—it would be a good idea to start out with a quick-and-dirty means of putting out fires during the first two years of construction while laying the framework for a comprehensive fire-fighting, communications, and security system. This means your camp-construction team would have to consider questions like these:

- Can we get by with buckets of water and fire extinguishers for the first summer?

- Do we have a first-aid kit? Should we have fire shelters, and radios and flashlights to clip on our belts, just in case a few people stay behind to save the structures?

- Should we buy some pumps so we can squirt water at a grass fire?

- Should we put a water tank and pump in the back of a pickup truck?

- Can we drill a well? Can we pipe in our water? Does

The Story—Part 2

the location of the well affect our choice of septic tank and leach-field locations or pressure us to include composting toilets? Will there be a backup generator if the power goes out?

- Can we tie our swimming pool into our fire-protection system?

- Do we need fire insurance?

- Can we cover our buildings with fire-protective foam if we have to evacuate in a hurry? How much does a foam unit cost?

- What kind of landscaping should we put in? Fast-growing pines? Ground covers? What if they escape into the forest and crowd out native plants?

- What is our evacuation plan in case of fire? Should we have a hand-cranked siren or just ring the camp bell in the event of a nighttime fire? What about false alarms?

- Can we put the utilities underground for esthetic reasons?

- Can we exist off the power grid? Could we dam up the creek and install a small hydrogenerator?

- Are there archeological sites that should be preserved?

Good luck with your camp. I hope my suggestions help you make it as safe as possible.

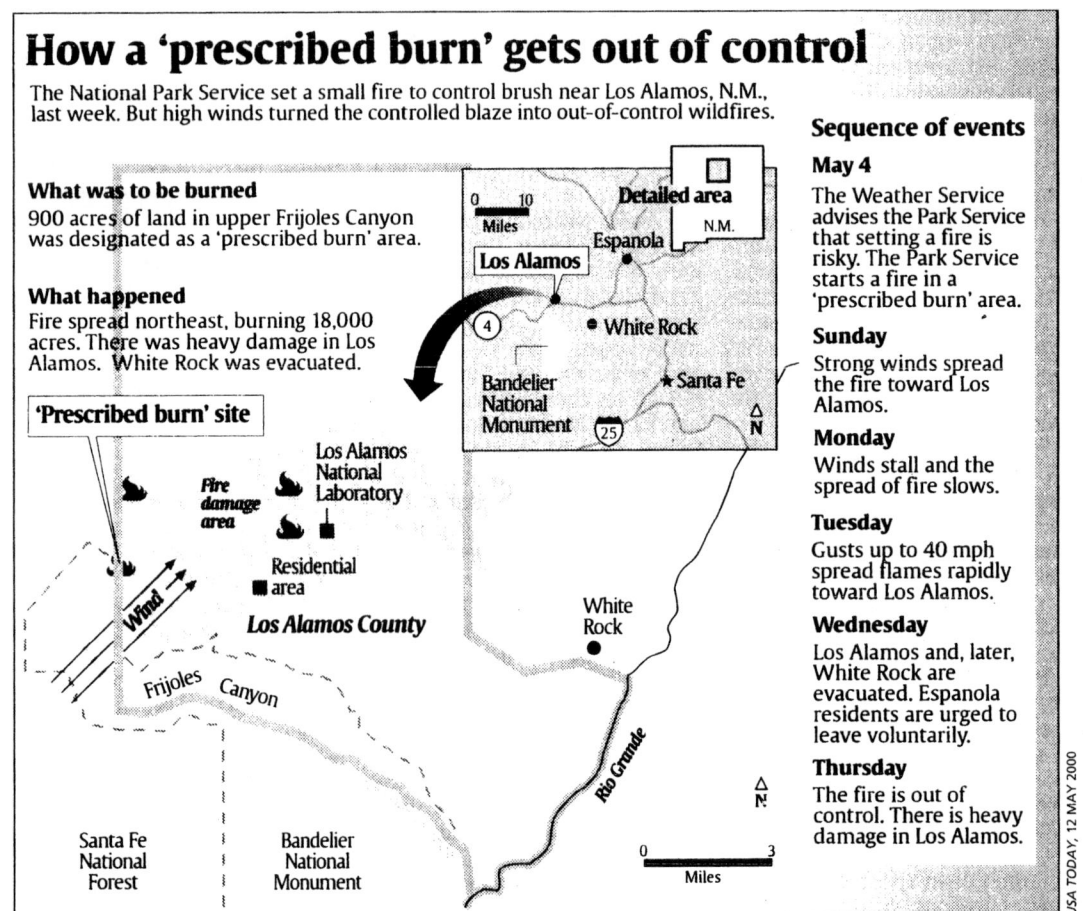

IN THE NEWS

How a 'prescribed burn' gets out of control

The National Park Service set a small fire to control brush near Los Alamos, N.M., last week. But high winds turned the controlled blaze into out-of-control wildfires.

What was to be burned
900 acres of land in upper Frijoles Canyon was designated as a 'prescribed burn' area.

What happened
Fire spread northeast, burning 18,000 acres. There was heavy damage in Los Alamos. White Rock was evacuated.

Sequence of events

May 4
The Weather Service advises the Park Service that setting a fire is risky. The Park Service starts a fire in a 'prescribed burn' area.

Sunday
Strong winds spread the fire toward Los Alamos.

Monday
Winds stall and the spread of fire slows.

Tuesday
Gusts up to 40 mph spread flames rapidly toward Los Alamos.

Wednesday
Los Alamos and, later, White Rock are evacuated. Espanola residents are urged to leave voluntarily.

Thursday
The fire is out of control. There is heavy damage in Los Alamos.

USA TODAY, 12 MAY 2000

IN THE NEWS

Experts defend controlled fires

Burns help keep forests healthy

By Traci Watson
USA TODAY

As incredible as it may seem that the government would deliberately set a fire, it does so routinely as a matter of environmental policy and to reduce fire risk.

The people who manage the USA's public lands, such as the national parks, say intentional fires are an essential tool in keeping forests and other ecosystems healthy.

Land managers don't defend the setting of the fire that gave rise to the inferno in Los Alamos, N.M., but they do defend the practice.

"As expensive as that fire will end up being, if we keep following this policy of fire exclusion, then we'll continue to have larger and more intense fires and more of them," says Ron Wakimoto, professor of forestry at the University of Montana-Missoula.

Western lands used to burn as often as every seven to nine years, going up in flames from lightning or fires set by Native Americans.

Then, around the turn of the 20th century, Westerners started putting fires out with a vengeance. Decades of extinguishing even the smallest fires have led to buildups of underbrush and small trees in the nation's forests and grasslands.

The result, experts agree, is a dry, overgrown landscape that makes the perfect tinder for lightning strikes, cigarette butts or carelessly banked campfires.

When Interior Secretary Bruce Babbitt, 61, was growing up in the West, "the motto was 'immediate suppression at all times and at any cost,'" he recalls. Babbitt worked on Western fire lines as a young man. "We got pretty successful at it, but the fires started getting bigger and more dangerous."

Since then, scientists have reached a consensus that the way to fight fire is with fire. Over the past decade, the intentional blazes known either as controlled burns or prescribed fires have become increasingly common. The federal government lights roughly 2.5 million acres ablaze every year, and state governments and private landowners also have turned to controlled burns.

Fire crews set flame to Virginia oak forests, Illinois prairies, Arizona pinyon scrub and Florida pines. Experts say the practice helps:

▶ Clear diseased trees.
▶ Make room for wildlife.
▶ Restore natural conditions, such as tall, widely spaced ponderosa pine groves.
▶ Encourage growth of certain vegetation, such as conifers whose cones need fire to open.

When land managers consider starting a fire, their goal is to keep it within a certain perimeter. There are three considerations: vegetation, topography of the land and weather, says James Agee, a forestry professor at the University of Washington.

Federal fire managers are required to write a "burn plan." It includes the fire's goals and the number of firefighters and amount of equipment that must be on hand to control it and, if need be, put it out.

The burn plan also details what the temperature, wind speed, humidity and fuel moisture must be before the fire can be started, says Denny Truesdale, assistant fire and aviation director for the U.S. Forest Service. When those conditions are reached, the fire can be set.

There's one more element that can help make for a successful fire: exactly how it's set. "A lot of times, the real skill and art of prescribed fire is the ignition pattern," Agee says. Fire managers can set fires against the wind to make them burn more slowly or with the wind to make them burn faster.

It is relatively rare for a controlled fire to "escape." The National Park Service estimates that since its controlled burn program began in 1968, only 38 of 3,746 prescribed fires have gone wrong. But it's safer to set controlled fires than to do nothing, officials say.

"There will always be forest fires," Babbitt says. But, he adds, those who take care of the land have realized that fire is "the safest way to fireproof a forest."

USA TODAY, 12 MAY 2000

The Story—Part 2

Discovery File

Oxygen: Who Needs It?

You need oxygen. Animals need oxygen. And fires need oxygen.

Oxygen is one of the three sides of the fire triangle (heat and fuel form the other two). Without oxygen to feed it, a fire will not burn.

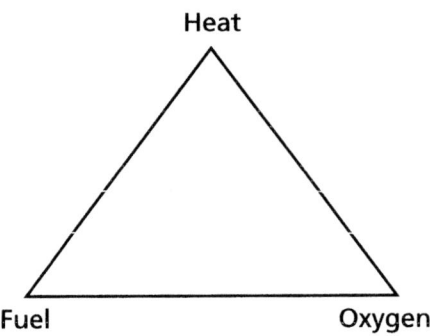

You can test this yourself by putting a beaker or glass jar over a burning candle. What happens? The flame uses up the oxygen inside the glass, and the fire stops burning.

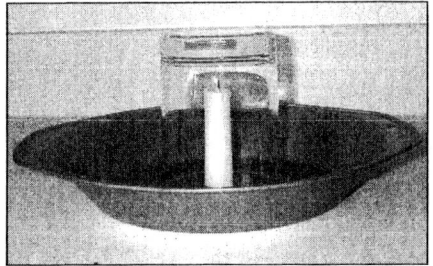

Unfortunately, it is a little harder to deprive a burning house or forest of oxygen. In fact, when firefighters first arrive on the scene of a burning building, they punch holes in the windows or walls, which has the effect of letting in a rush of oxygen that feeds the fire. But before they can fight the fire, they must create ways for the smoke and toxic gases to escape.

In a forest fire, strong winds will whip up a fire and intensify it. If they reach a fire early enough, firefighters can sometimes smother it with chemicals. But once a fire is raging, strong, gusting winds provide the oxygen it needs to grow and spread.

Oxygen, of course, is essential to almost every form of life on Earth. Both plants and animals use oxygen to break down their food in a process called *respiration*.

Oxygen Throughout History

Did you know that Earth's atmosphere hasn't always contained oxygen? Today, oxygen makes up about 21% of the air on Earth. But at one time, our atmosphere was quite different. Evidence suggests that in the distant past there was no oxygen in the atmosphere, and carbon dioxide was at much higher levels than it is today.

Earth is about 4.5 billion years old, but the first free oxygen appeared only about 2 billion years ago. It was not until plants evolved, and the process of photosynthesis began, that carbon dioxide levels started to drop and oxygen levels began to rise.

Some scientists today have expressed concern that CO_2 levels in the atmosphere, along with other greenhouse gases like methane and nitrous oxide, are again rising. Some say to alarming levels.

Oxygen, the most common chemical element in our world, is invisible, lacking color, taste, or smell. No wonder early scientists didn't know what it was. Oxygen was first isolated in the eighteenth century, independently by two scientists. In about 1773, Swedish chemist and pharmacist Karl Scheele discovered oxygen. Around the same time in England, Joseph Priestly discovered oxygen—and he published his results before Scheele.

Priestly was investigating the gases involved in burning when he made his great discoveries. He also discovered that plants change the air around them. In his experiments, Priestly burned candles enclosed in jars. It was first believed that a candle released "phlogisticated air" as it burned. When Priestly put a plant in the jar of carbon dioxide that had collected from a burning candle, the air became "dephlogisticated" (actually, the plant took in the CO_2 and gave out oxygen in its place). What Priestly had discovered were two gases vital to respiration and photosynthesis: carbon dioxide and oxygen.

24   Fire!

People living in the late Middle Ages and even into the eighteenth century believed that something called "phlogiston" was released when things burned. In 1774, French chemist Antoine Lavoisier ruled out the existence of phlogiston when he demonstrated the role of oxygen in a combustion reaction and gave oxygen its name.

Oxygen's Role in Fire

When substances react with oxygen, they are said to be *oxidized*. When fossil fuels like coal and oil are ignited, they are burned, or oxidized. A fire in a burning building is an example of very rapid oxidation: combustion, or fire.

By oxidizing certain compounds, your body releases energy. You eat food, which is then burned, or oxidized, during respiration. Without the fuel you get from food, your body would not have energy to function or sustain itself.

More than 200 years ago, Priestly realized his candles would not burn inside jars of carbon dioxide. Some of today's fire extinguishers use foam or carbon dioxide gas to smother a fire and deprive it of oxygen, thus stopping the oxidation reaction.

In a fire, the amount of life-giving oxygen diminishes. People trapped in a burning room often do not realize that their judgment becomes impaired by this lack of oxygen. Get out of a burning building and away from fire immediately, before the impairment sets in. Call the fire department from a neighbor's house. Whatever you do, don't try to go back until the fire department says it's safe. Many people who want to rush back into a burning building are suffering from oxygen deprivation and have lost their ability to think clearly.

Oxygen itself can be hazardous. Hospitals and homes where oxygen is being used for health reasons know to warn visitors about the extreme flammability of this most precious element.

IN THE NEWS

Rain forecast gives Alaska some hope

By Steve Marshall
USA TODAY

Wind-stoked wildfires continued scorching Alaska while residents awaited rain forecast for tonight to help contain a blaze that has burned an area larger than Boston or Miami.

No deaths or serious injuries have been reported in the what Gov. Tony Knowles called the "most devastating fire in Alaska's history."

The fire consumed 42,000 acres, tripling in size in a matter of hours and casting smoke over Anchorage 50 miles to the north. It has destroyed hundreds of houses and forced evacuation of 3,000 people.

Some weary residents were allowed back to their homes Thursday to retrieve vehicles and pets.

Like a tornado, the fire was capricious in what it damaged.

"It burned right under my Camaro, and the paint's not even touched," Bill Summerville said.

Since Monday, winds of up to 40 mph have whipped the fire into 200-foot plumes that spread rapidly in the dry conditions.

Knowles announced late Thursday that an office is being established in Wasilla to help victims.

The center will provide residents with information about state, federal and other disaster assistance available once recovery begins.

More than 1,250 firefighters, many from other states, joined 300 of their colleagues Thursday to combat the fire.

Working 12-hour shifts, the firefighters were reinforced by 10 helicopters and five water-bomber aircraft.

Daily firefighting efforts cost an estimated $1 million, said Knowles spokesman Bob King.

The Federal Emergency Management Agency is paying 70% of the firefighting bill, spokesman Morrie Goodman said.

Officials estimate the number of homes destroyed at between 150 and 500. Property damage totals $40 million.

The Parks Highway, the main road from Anchorage to Fairbanks, has been closed intermittently because of heavy smoke and fire.

The area is a popular weekend getaway for Anchorage residents and has experienced explosive growth in recent years. Officials believe the fire was started by fireworks or a campfire.

Another fire near Central, a small town about 400 miles northeast of Anchorage, continued to burn. It has burned more than 5,000 acres, officials said, but no structures were reported lost.

Another home gone: Flames engulf a home Wednesday near Big Lake, Alaska. Up to 500 homes may have been destroyed.
By Bob Hallinen, Anchorage Daily News via AP

Discovery File

Fuel: What Matters to a Fire

It may seem obvious, but fuel is critical to a fire. Fuel is the material that reacts with oxygen and heat to burn.

Fuels can be solid, liquid, or gas. Your car runs on a liquid fuel, gasoline, derived from petroleum. When gasoline combusts, the liquid itself does not burn; the vapors do. Wood and paper become the fuel for many fires, accidental or intentional. Natural gas is a fuel that may heat your home and the hot water for your showers.

If you've ever watched a house go up in flames, think about the various fuels the fire feeds on and consumes. Everything from newspapers, plastic toys, and wooden doors to fabrics in furniture, clothes, and bedding will burn. A fire isn't especially choosy when it comes to fuel; almost everything in your home will burn eventually, except bricks, pipes, and water. Each material has its own *kindling point,* or temperature at which it will ignite. And some fuels burn faster than others.

It's often said that an old building is a "tinderbox." The word comes from the old-fashioned metal box that held tinder (wood scraps) people used to help start a fire. Before matches were invented, people used flint (a hard rock) and steel to ignite fires. Striking flint against steel produced sparks that set tinder on fire. So, an old house of dry wood just waiting to go up in flames is like tinder waiting to burn. In older houses made of post-and-beam construction, there were no firewalls or insulation between walls to slow the spread of fire.

Today's homes, although made more fire resistant by the use of less-flammable materials, have many volatile fuel sources. Some of the newer plastics used in appliances are easily ignited and have been shown to be a hazard when near a faulty electrical connection. A test of an office workstation showed that it went from open flame to flashover condition in 7 minutes.

One of the most critical problems in American forests is the buildup of fuel on forest floors. For decades, the policy among firefighters and park personnel was to extinguish all fires. A huge surplus of fuel in the form of dead wood, bark, leaves, twigs, branches, and logs accumulated over the last century, especially since the fire-suppression policy went into effect. The excess fuel load in Yellowstone was blamed for contributing to the disastrous fires of 1988.

In some areas of the West, local laws require that people create a fire safety zone around their homes so that a fire would have less fuel. Homeowners are also encouraged to plant fire-resistant vegetation where fires are a constant threat. A person in a typical home has less than 2 minutes to escape, so the danger of fire is one that should not be taken lightly. One way to prevent a fire is to reduce the available fuel, inside and out.

Fossil Fuels

Fossil fuels were formed millions of years ago, when time and pressure acted on the remains of tiny dead animals and plants—converting the organic matter to coal, petroleum, and natural gas. The first widely used fossil fuel was coal; coal also can be used to produce a form of gas that was used to heat and light homes and factories 100 years ago. The fossil fuel that rules the planet today is oil, because so many products are made from it, including gasoline, heating oil, kerosene, and jet fuel.

Over the millennia, people have used many kinds of fuels to produce heat and light. Where wood and coal were scarce, people used peat—compressed, decomposing plant material in swamps, a primitive form of coal. On the American prairies, people burned buffalo chips. Native Americans burned what they called "rock oil," crude oil that bubbled out of the ground.

One problem with all fossil fuels is that they are not renewable—they can be used only once. The search is on for clean, safe, effective, alternative fuels—including nuclear, solar, and geothermal—because at some point in the future, Earth's supply of fossil fuels will run out.

SCIENCE ACTIVITY

Get Out!

Purpose
To build a scale model of a room with several common fire hazards, group several rooms together, and plan three escape routes in case of fire.

Background
Many children do not have first-hand knowledge of the fire hazards in their own homes. Most are also unfamiliar with fire safety and evacuation procedures. As an expert in fire safety, you have been asked to design a classroom display that will be shown to elementary school students during National Fire Safety Week.

Materials
For each pair:
- shoe box
- markers
- paper
- construction paper
- clay

Procedure
1. List typical fire hazards found around the home.
2. Work with your partner to create a shoe-box diorama of any room in a house or an apartment, complete with all the fire hazards you can fit into it. Use clay and paper to construct your diorama inside the shoe box, as well as any other materials you can find and incorporate.
3. Make a list of fire safety procedures appropriate for the room.
4. Build a model of a house or an apartment by grouping your room model together with rooms from several other fire safety experts.
5. Devise an evacuation plan for this "home," including three escape routes.

Conclusion
1. With your partner, prepare a presentation showing fire hazards in the room model you built. Gear your presentation to an audience of first and second graders.
2. Compose a song the elementary students can sing to help them remember safety precautions and evacuation procedures.
3. Show your presentation to your class, and teach them the song you have written.

The Story—Part 2   27

ON THE JOB

Fire Information Officer

**SUE CONSOLO-MURPHY
YELLOWSTONE NATIONAL
PARK**

Sue has worked in Yellowstone National Park for 15 of her 20 years in the field. The fires of 1988 were a vivid event for Sue, whose job at the time was giving campfire programs as part of her work as a park naturalist.

Most of us started out as firefighters. The first class you take teaches you how to go out safely and dig fire line and use your muscles. Just like everyone else, that's where I started. This usually happens when you're young and have lots of energy and can be gone for three weeks fighting one fire and then off for another week to fight another fire. And you make money—lots of students pay their way through college fighting fires. As you get a little older and advance in the fire organization, you realize you don't want to dig fire line forever. It's exhausting, it's smoky, and you realize you want to do other things—keep the food coming in, run the radio, predict the weather.

I started working for the U.S. Forest Service in Utah and have done many different kinds of duty, including working in the Badlands, where I set prescribed fires in grasslands. These are very different from forest fires. You plan a fire for the day, start the fire, do your burn, and go home. Those were very hot fires. Many fires I've been on have been cold and boring. Half the time you're freezing.

When there's a fire in the forest, everybody goes to help. There's no media. You bag your own lunch. On one fire, they needed someone to operate a radio in the truck. So instead of building fireline, I spent the night in the truck, sending messages back. That's how I went from digging fire lines to working in fire information.

An important part of the fire organization is providing information. If your regular job is working in public affairs or as a park naturalist and doing campfire programs, it's natural for someone to say, "You'd be good fire information officer. You're used to talking to people, it doesn't make you nervous, and you know how to do interviews with the press."

Like most of the park naturalists in 1988, that's what we were drafted to do. For a while we all tried to do our normal jobs, but as the summer went on, it became clear there was no such thing as normal that year.

The name recognition of Yellowstone brought much more media attention than a normal big fire would. We often point out that of 250 fires in the Yellowstone Ecosystem that year, only one fifth of them were in the park. The big story, of course, is Yellowstone. Two years later, visitors driving through some of the most scorched roads in the park still expected to see 300-foot walls of flame. Even the reporters showed a lack of knowledge about fire behavior. Most people know very little about fire ecology.

If you are going to set up a camp, go back to some basics: Fire needs a source of ignition and fuel to keep it burning. What does that mean in a forest? Matches are a source of ignition. If it's rainy, some people pour fuel on the fire. Try to think about what would happen in this situation, and connect it to a wildfire. If a fire is creeping along and hits a source of fuel—like a cabin with a propane tank in it, or someone's lantern, or a natural source like sap—what will happen?

When you learn about tinder or kindling and how to build a fire, you'll learn about building a fire up to the point where it can take a bigger log. That's exactly what happens with a wildfire.

A wildfire doesn't start in big, fat logs. It starts with tinder and kindling. A lightning strike usually occurs in an old, dead tree that is rotten and starting to

28   Fire!

fall apart. It has little crumbly bits of fuel. Or the fire starts in the *duff,* as it's called—the litter or dried leaves on the forest floor. If materials are dry and plentiful, a fire will get going. It begins to generate its own heat. Then along comes a gust of wind and spreads fire into thicker tinder—and that's exactly what happens in the forest.

Fires always start rather slowly. Until 1988, many fires were allowed to burn in the park. But as the summer of 1988 went on, and the winds came and the fires progressed toward the park boundary where they threatened a community, and conditions grew drier and drier, we were beaten by statistics. The odds were, in another given year, rain would have dampened down the fire. Lack of precipitation, back-to-back wind events, the accumulation of fuel that kept getting drier and drier—all combined to produce the fires of 1988.

After the fire, Yellowstone, like other parks, had to rewrite its fire-management plan and tighten its fire prescriptions. Now we suppress some fires we would have let burn. We're required to keep track of more daily fire data. We monitor the weather and the fuel-moisture loads closely and add this information to an ongoing database. We plug this into a nationwide computer network that keeps people up to date on fires and the resources to fight them.

The fire provided an exciting event for scientists to study in the years after, as they track recovery to learn how the whole ecosystem comes back. We might not have a major fire like this for another 200 years, but meanwhile, as the database grows, we'll learn what we need to know to be prepared for the next one.

STUDENT VOICES

The fires were really bad because it was really hot. Fire can spread and get out of control very easily, especially with the trees and other things popping.

I was at the high school with my mom and dad when we heard that they had evacuated our street. Dad went to our house, and the fire was across the lake. He got my granny and my sisters and brothers out. They were all crying.

We stayed at a motel while our house burnt down, and it felt really bad.

We are going to rebuild our home in the same area. We have already cleared the lot. The plants are growing back. The palmettos are already green, and the trees are starting to get green at the top.

PAISLEY MAJEWSKI
PALM COAST, FL

THE STORY—PART 3

Fire in America: The Early Years

No one knows for certain how many fires burned during the thousands of years that Native Americans alone occupied the North American continent. But we do know that Indians periodically set fires to clear grasslands.

For the colonies founded along the Atlantic shore of North America, however, fires were a major threat to survival. And the building materials themselves were the worst fire hazards. With most buildings in the early settlements made of wood, it's not surprising that fire was a frequent problem. And when a fire came to the American colonies, people could do little more than watch and wait for it to burn out or for rain or snow to extinguish it.

Jamestown, 1608 The recorded history of America began with a fire. During the first winter in the colony of Jamestown—the first permanent English settlement in America— fires burned nearly every building. Out of the ashes, Jamestown was rebuilt.

Fire also swept through the Pilgrim settlement in Plymouth, Massachusetts, almost devastating that colony too. Diaries from Plymouth tell us that the chimneys were the main cause of fires. At the time, chimneys were made of wood, lined and covered with mud or mortar. As this protective covering dried out, a wooden chimney would be directly exposed to flames. The inside walls of chimneys also became coated with a black tar. When the wood of a chimney or the tar on its walls finally caught fire, sparks would spew onto the thatched roofs, and fire would quickly engulf the building.

A modern chimney

Note: The buildup of tar and creosote makes chimneys a potential fire hazard even today. Chimneys must be regularly cleaned and inspected.

Boston, 1631 After a series of fires in the colonies, the first fire regulations were established. The new laws stated that no one could build chimneys out of wood or cover their houses with thatch (leaves or straw).

New Amsterdam, 1647–48 New Amsterdam— later called New York—also suffered many chimney fires in its wooden buildings. Organized fire fighting did not exist at the time; putting out fires was a volunteer effort. If people saw a fire, they would alert nearby homeowners. Neighbors would grab their leather fire buckets and use them to scoop water from whatever source was handy. Then they moved as close to the fire as they could stand, and tossed water onto it.

Peter Stuyvesant, the governor of New Amsterdam, brought order to fire fighting. He declared thatched roofs and wooden chimneys on new buildings illegal and began to introduce other fire regulations. He also appointed the country's first fire wardens. One of their jobs was chimney inspection. Because of the new laws, New York did not have a major fire for almost 100 years.

Late seventeenth century In spite of fire codes, cities such as Boston continued to experience devastating fires. Frequent fires finally forced the people to establish tougher laws and building codes. They also tried to organize their fire-fighting efforts. Bucket brigades—in which one person passed a bucket of water to the next, and so on down a line—were the first attempt. But bucket brigades

30   *Fire!*

were not very effective. In 1676, Boston bought its first fire engine, a pumper made in London. The first fire company in America was now at work.

Boston had an even more serious fire hazard than flammable building materials: *firebugs,* or *arsonists,* people who started fires intentionally.

Early eighteenth century As cities such as Philadelphia grew, planners began to design cities in a gridiron pattern, with wide, straight streets rather than the crooked, narrow streets of the older European-style cities. Benjamin Franklin encouraged the first volunteer fire-fighting association in Philadelphia. Other cities followed. Famous Americans who were volunteer firefighters include George Washington, Thomas Jefferson, and Paul Revere.

The American Revolution You could say that "fire" helped to ignite the Boston Massacre of 1770. A mob of Bostonians threw rocks and ice balls at British sentries and then began running through the streets crying out "Fire!" This brought more people into the streets. Confusion grew into riot, and eventually British soldiers began to shoot. The deaths of five townspeople was one of the events that lead to the American Revolution. And during the Revolutionary War, both sides used fire as a weapon.

Nineteenth century Being a firefighter was an honor in the nineteenth century. Volunteer fire companies were manned by the highest-ranking men in town. But despite the firefighters' dedication, the weapons they used to fight fires remained primitive—leather buckets, axes, and pumpers that could shoot water 75 feet at most. Fire hydrants, if they existed, were made of wood. Fire hose was improved and made more reliable, but the firemen themselves still pulled the wagons carrying their equipment.

The most infamous event during the War of 1812 occurred when the British burned Washington, D.C., almost completely destroying the Capitol building.

Many cities experienced large, destructive fires during this century. New Orleans, Pittsburgh, St. Louis, New York, San Francisco—each had its own "great fire." Many cities were still made of wood and canvas buildings; fires were inevitable. Big fires were even considered entertainment for tourists who would stay in town to watch the latest spectacle unfold.

Unfortunately, it often took a big fire with many lives lost to force change. An 1860 New York City fire is a good example. Tenement buildings were being built much taller than ladders could reach, and they had no fire escapes. Although a fire in one of these buildings resulted in tremendous loss of life, it helped to change the laws. After that experience, all apartment buildings were required to have fire escapes.

The Civil War Fire played a large role in this war too, from the fires of draft riots to General Sherman's infamous burning of Atlanta.

A blazing structure crumbles to the ground

DISCOVERY FILE

Fire Myths

To our ancestors, fire was magic. They worshipped it, feared it, and relied on it for their existence. But they did not understand fire's properties or what made it work. They couldn't explain where fire came from, so they created myths to explain its origin and its power.

A mythological bird known to ancient Greeks as the Phoenix was sacred to the sun god. This eagle-like bird with red and gold feathers was said to have a 500-year life. At the end of that time, the bird built its own funeral pyre and set itself on fire. Out of the ashes a new Phoenix would be born. This cycle would be repeated every 500 years.

The ancient Greeks explained the origins of fire this way: Prometheus, a Titan, stole fire from rival gods and gave it to the people, along with the arts and sciences. In retaliation, the gods gave Pandora's box, with all its troubles, to civilization.

Vulcan, the ancient Roman god of fire, was said to forge weapons underground in his workshop. A smoking volcano was a sign that Vulcan was hard at work; an erupting volcano meant he was angry.

In what is now called Hawaii, the Polynesians had their own volcanic legend about the fire goddess, Pele. They believed that Pele lived in the crater of the still-active volcano Mauna Loa on the island of Hawaii. The volcano's eruptions were blamed on Pele's jealous rages. Pele had a rival in the fire goddess Poliahu, whose home was believed to be Mauna Kea, the now-dormant volcano, also on Hawaii.

Fire was supremely important to ancient cultures. The discovery of the usefulness of fire, probably following a forest fire caused by lightning, led to major changes in the way people lived. They could now have heat and light. They could cook their food instead of eating it raw—and cooked meat has more interesting flavors than raw meat. They could frighten away predators. They could use fire to clear land, in *slash-and-burn agriculture,* which is still used by many cultures around the world. With agriculture came primitive civilization. Eventually, fire would be used to bake clay pots, smelt metal, and make glass.

No one can say for certain when the first fires were used, as the archeological evidence does not tell us whether ancient fires were accidental or deliberate. Some evidence for the deliberate use of fire has been found at sites in Africa dating to 1.5 million years ago. Evidence of hearths can be dated to about 500,000 years ago.

Native Americans in what is now North America recognized the benefits and dangers of fire. The Paiute Indians told a tale of Coyote, the Fire Bringer, who with a boy brought fire from the Burning Mountain to the Paiute people, a brave deed celebrated in many stories.

American Indians cleared large areas of brush and prairies using wildfire. They built their homes in the center of the clearings they made, after they were free of flammable materials. These clearings also allowed the people to keep an eye on anyone who approached. Indians also used fire to hunt, setting fire to areas of forests and forcing game to run from the fires.

When the first Pilgrims arrived on our shores, they used fire in similar ways. They burned the forests to clear land for farming and to protect themselves from attacks by Indians. For the settlers in North America, wood was the primary fuel.

As pioneers moved across the continent, they logged and burned forests in their paths. Not until the late nineteenth century did anyone worry about saving the trees. In 1872, Yellowstone National Park became the first land in the world protected and designated as a park. Under the Creative Act of 1891, the U.S. began to set aside forest land. President Benjamin Harrison created the first forest reserves (later called national forests), and by 1897 the United States had set aside 20 million acres. In 1905, the U.S. Forest Service was created. One of its goals was protecting forests from wildfire.

Over the millennia, as the technology of fire use and management advanced, so did civilization. But it would take tens of thousands of years to move from using charcoal and wood as fuel to harnessing the energy in coal and oil.

Ancient people may not have understood the physics or chemistry of fire, but they were awed by its power. Fire played a central role in many religions and cultures. Fire is still a powerful symbol in our own modern ceremonies; for example, the Olympic flame and perpetual flames still burn in celebration of events and remembrance of people. And images of fire throughout literature, songs, and art continue to inspire and provoke us, as in the words of Robert Frost: *"Some say the world will end in fire."*

STUDENT VOICES

The fire was really, really bad. It destroyed 23 homes in Seminole Woods, and mine was one of them. It didn't destroy businesses, but did burn the woods and fields. When I first saw it, I was really scared.

It is a bad feeling to be evacuated. I didn't know if my house was going to go or to stay. I didn't know if the fire department was going to come soon and wet down my house so it wouldn't get burned.

My dad almost died in the fire. He was squirting down the house, and the fire was two feet from him. He heard a "swoosh" sound and a bunch of trees dropped near him. He tried to go around to the right of the house but there was fire over there, and then he went the other way and he couldn't go there either. He was trapped until a police officer came from out of the woods and saw him going back and forth and helped him get out.

I felt really, really mad because the fire department did not get to my house in time. They could have been better prepared. Don't trust the fire companies if they say you will be okay and won't be evacuated. When you see a fire, take your stuff and get out of there. The fire was coming down both sides of the highway and we almost did not get away.

BARBARA DiMARTINO
FLAGLER BEACH, FL

The Story—Part 3

Discovery File

Put 'em Out or Let 'em Burn?

It used to be the practice in this country to put out forest fires as quickly as possible. But that policy was based on a lack of understanding of the role of fire in a forest ecosystem.

Today we know that fire, while dangerous and destructive, can also be beneficial. It rids the forest of dead wood. It enriches the soil. It reduces fuel loads. It encourages diversity of animal and plant life. And some species of plants and trees depend on the heat of a fire to release their seeds.

The first fire-suppression policy was enacted in 1872, the year that Yellowstone became America's first national park. Park policy required that all fires were to be put out. However, until fire-fighting technology improved after World War II, few fires could actually be extinguished.

In the late 1960s, the thinking about fire began to change. There began to be a growing recognition that wildfires are one of the ways a forest renews itself and that putting them out disrupts a natual cycle in the forest. Perhaps total fire suppression was not the best strategy. In 1972, Yellowstone officials introduced a new and revolutionary *natural-burning policy:* fires started by lightning would be allowed to burn unless they threatened people or structures. Fires set by people—either by accident or on purpose—would be fought aggressively.

Ironically, the 1972 policy may have come too late. The

Since his introduction in 1944, firefighters and the public alike have supported the message of Smokey Bear: Only YOU Can Prevent Forest Fires. Rescued from a forest fire in New Mexico during the 1950s, an orphaned bear cub named Smokey became a living mascot for this forest-fire prevention campaign.

The campaign raised awareness of the need to prevent fires. Because 88% of all fires are caused by humans (and 47% of all acreage burned is from human-caused fires), Smokey Bear's message is still valid today. See the official Smokey Bear Web page of the U.S. Department of Agriculture (www.smokeybear.com).

situation actually grew worse as leaves, dead wood, branches, twigs, and bark continued to build up on the forest floor.

When the fires first started in May 1988, officials decided to let them burn. But that summer had been very hot and dry, and the fuel load was enormous. The wildfires quickly got out of control.

In mid July, park officials changed their minds and decided to put out all the fires. But it was too late. The fires had become catastrophic, burning out of control until the rain and snow arrived.

A firestorm of controversy over fire management blazed in the years following the Yellowstone fires. Critics blamed the natural-burning policy in place in 1988 for contributing to the fires; they said fire officials should have stopped the fires immediately. Other people argued that the natural-burning policy was ecologically beneficial. Still others criticized the fire-suppression policy in place for a century, which led to a buildup of fuel in the forest.

The Yellowstone fires of 1988 have helped bring about a broader understanding of the role of fire in a forest. The great fires were a big experiment from which scientists could investigate causes and consequences of large-scale fires. After decades of a policy that suppressed wildfires, fire managers now recognize that some fires are beneficial and selected fires are allowed to burn. However, since the Yellowstone fires, fire managers have made some changes to their overall fire-management plans.

Another technique of fire management that is being used more today is the *prescribed* or *controlled burn*. A controlled burn is a carefully planned fire, set to clear out dead wood when conditions are right, before it catches fire during a drought. Prescribed burns help reduce the fuel load, clear out logging debris, and enrich the soil. Some fire ecologists point out that had controlled burns been used in the decades before 1988, the fuel load would have been lower.

But no one knows for sure. Past suppression policies, along with wind and weather, did result in an unusual set of conditions that set the stage for the fires that followed.

Debate continues over the most effective policy for forest-fire management. The key point that fire managers and the U.S. Forest Service emphasize today is forest health. Of course, a fire that endangers human civilization must be fought. And although this happens in Southern California every fire season, some ecologists argue that people should not be allowed to build in these fire-prone areas.

Devising a balanced fire-management program is a continuing issue that affects many areas of the United States, not just the West. Debate on the issue continues.

IN THE NEWS

N.M. fire forces 500 to flee

Started Thursday: Firefighters battle on Monday a blaze that officials set at Bandelier National Monument in New Mexico to get rid of excess underbrush. Fed by low humidity and high winds, the fire scorched nearly 2,000 acres, forced 500 residents to evacuate and prompted the partial closure of the nuclear Los Alamos National Laboratory.

By Josh Stephenson, Albuquerque Journal, via AP
USA TODAY, 9 MAY 2000

IN THE NEWS

N.M. fire claims could be difficult

By Traci Watson
USA TODAY

Residents of Los Alamos, N.M., began returning to their homes Monday, five days after a 44,000-acre wildfire forced 25,000 people to flee. But it will take much longer to make the victims "whole."

With the wildfire only 28% contained, federal officials are vowing to do just that — a promise that can be fulfilled only with an act of Congress or a drawn-out claims process filled with red tape.

More than 400 families have lost their homes to the Cerro Grande wildfire, which was started May 4 by National Park Service workers trying to clear brush in a so-called controlled burn.

Like most disaster victims, the Los Alamos families are eligible for aid from the Federal Emergency Management Agency: up to 18 months of temporary housing and $10,000 grants for home repairs. President Clinton has declared a disaster area, which enables victims to seek aid ranging from jobless benefits to legal counseling.

But unlike tornadoes and other acts of God, the Cerro Grande fire may have been someone's fault:

By J. Pat Carter, AP

28% contained: Blue Ridge firefighter Barry Kennedy rests after battling the Cerro Grande blaze Monday near Los Alamos, N.M.

the government's. Victims can try to get more cash from federal coffers, but they must fight their way through extensive paperwork.

Making the claims process even more formidable, a decades-old law called the Federal Tort Claims Act shields the government from liability for a wide range of actions. The controlled burn that started the Cerro Grande fire might be included among them, officials say.

However, Interior Secretary Bruce Babbitt told CNN Sunday, "If we were negligent, we pay."

Interior Department officials say special legislation would be the fastest and easiest way to compensate victims. It would spell out which losses could be reimbursed and the steps victims would have to take. The law could also include compensation funds.

Federal officials say one precedent for such a law was legislation passed after the Teton Dam in Idaho burst in 1976, killing 11 people and destroying 4,000 homes and businesses. An investigation revealed the government had built the dam despite warnings from geologists that the site was hazardous. Congress appropriated $200 million for the victims.

Victims of a similar incident in Lewiston, Calif., hope Los Alamos residents get a break from Congress. Dozens of Lewiston families lost their homes in 1999 after a controlled burn ignited by the Interior Department raged into town. The government has admitted liability, but the victims are still fighting their way through the claims process, trying to list their possessions down to the last fork.

Contributing: Frank Santiago

Fire!

IN THE NEWS

U.S. takes blame in N.M. fire

Fireproofing plan studied for West

By Patrick O'Driscoll
USA TODAY

With blunt self-criticism, the government took formal responsibility Thursday for the wildfire that destroyed hundreds of homes last week in Los Alamos, N.M.

In what Interior Secretary Bruce Babbitt called "an unflinching appraisal" of the disaster, a team of fire investigators concluded that carelessness and "critical mistakes" up and down the chain of command led to the inferno, which forced more than 25,000 people to flee.

National Park Service crews in Bandelier National Monument, south of Los Alamos, started the fire intentionally May 4 to clear brush. However, conditions were unacceptably dry and windy, and they lost control of their "controlled burn." It raced into national forest land next door and burned north, where it torched more than 220 homes and threatened Los Alamos National Laboratory, the birthplace of the atomic bomb.

The blaze, still burning in the forest Thursday but 60% contained, has consumed nearly 48,000 acres.

The White House said it is meeting with Congress to ensure that the fire's victims are compensated.

Babbitt, announcing the results of the investigation at a news conference in Santa Fe, said the park service's pre-fire analysis of the burn's complexity was "seriously flawed."

In an effort to "avoid the possibility of another Los Alamos," Babbitt also proposed on Thursday a sweeping program to fireproof the risky perimeter where urban sprawl meets scenic forests in other communities across the West.

He said such an "urban-wildland interface" initiative is being discussed by the USA's federal land agencies and Congress.

Fire investigators reported that officials:
▶ Didn't review the burning plan properly before it was approved.
▶ Ignored fire safety and hazards beyond the fire's intended boundaries.
▶ Failed to check wind forecasts.
▶ Didn't have adequate staff and equipment standing by to put out the fire.
▶ Didn't follow safety policies for firefighters and civilians.

"We have a special obligation ... to avoid the possibility of another Los Alamos," Babbitt said.

USA TODAY, 19 MAY 2000

STUDENT VOICES

In our neighborhood, the fire destroyed this one home. Sometimes when I go past it, I hate to look at it. My house got partially damaged and the neighbor's is all black, but there are plants growing back around my yard, and the grass is greener. The fields are also growing back. They said in the newspaper that they were going to knock down the burned trees and plant new ones.

While we were evacuated, I didn't want to get my parents mad but some nights I stayed out late instead of helping; I did things like play basketball to help keep my mind off things.

If fire is coming your way, I would water the house down, pack up your stuff, and leave.

MATTHEW DAVIDSON
PALM COAST, FL

The Story—Part 3

Discovery File

Kindling Point

The lowest temperature at which a substance will catch fire and continue to burn is known as its *kindling point,* or ignition temperature. Technically, the kindling point is the temperature at which the fuel easily combines with oxygen. Certain materials, like paper, have relatively low kindling points. Some fuels, like coal, must be heated for a while before they can burn. The chemical *white phosphorus* must be kept under water at room temperature or else it will explode into flames.

At right are the kindling points of some common materials. For the sake of comparison, some other measures are also shown on this temperature scale.

- –128.6°F lowest recorded temperature on Earth (Antarctica)
- 32°F water freezes
- 71°F rubbing alcohol (undiluted) burns
- 98.6°F human body's normal temperature
- 135.9°F highest recorded temperature on Earth (Libya)
- 212°F water boils at sea level
- 311°F rubber bands burn
- 360°F match head burns
- 375°F to 800°F wood burns
- 451°F paper burns
- 468°F cellophane burns
- 500°F to 800°F gasoline burns
- 620°F lead melts
- 850°F plastic credit cards burn
- 900°F to 1170°F a natural gas flame
- 1600°F steel burns
- 1940°F gold burns
- 2795°F iron melts
- 10,000°F surface temperature of the sun

38   Fire!

DISCOVERY FILE

The Ecology of Forest Fires

Every day more than 300 forest fires start in the United States. Do we put them all out? Or should we sit and watch the forests burn? How about setting fire to the forests on purpose? Which of these strategies is best for the health of our forests?

Ancient cultures may have had an intuition about the benefits of fire, but today we rely on experiments and scientific observations to confirm or deny our intuitions. The Yellowstone fires of 1988 gave fire ecologists—scientists who study the role of fire in nature—a natural laboratory for investigating these questions. Because of what we've learned from those fires, we have a better understanding of the role that fire plays in a healthy forest.

We now know that without periodic fires, a forest is at greater risk from disease, insects, and the high-intensity crown fires that jump from treetop to treetop and can destroy everything.

Small fires eliminate some of the leaves, dead wood, twigs, branches, and bark that accumulate on the forest floor. The unnatural *fuel load* that builds up in a forest where every fire is put out actually makes fires worse and more likely to burn out of control.

When pine trees are allowed to grow for 50 to 100 years, they become very tall and dense. When they block the sun, younger and shorter plants die. Without periodic fires to thin out the trees, the newer growth usually dies off completely.

Before Europeans settled on our continent, fires burned naturally. Trees were spaced farther apart, and some parklike grassy areas were common within the forests. The native peoples periodically set fires to clear out the underbrush, just as people do today in parts of Africa and Asia.

Another problem with very old pines is that they do not produce enough resin (sap) to keep insects from boring into them. The *mountain pine beetle* bores into the bark and kills the oldest trees. What remains are pockets of old, dead trees that can burn very quickly.

After a fire, plants grow back. Soil is actually enriched by a fire. Some plant species are even adapted to living with fire. Sequoias, for example, need heat to release their seeds.

After years of the United States' total fire-suppression policy, many forests are full of dead trees. Forests are losing some species. *Aspen,* a pioneer species that takes root after a fire, is declining throughout the Rocky Mountain West because other trees have taken over.

"Change is inherent in forest ecosystems, and fire is frequently the agent of this change," said forest ecologist Dr. Jason Greenlee, testifying in July 1997 before a House Agriculture Committee on forest health. "Scientists now know that the exclusion of fire from our landscapes has a myriad of well-documented, long-term impacts that are hard to see on a short time scale. . . . As long as wildlands remain, wildland fire will flourish."

The Story—Part 3

SCIENCE ACTIVITY

A Very Extinguished Career

Purpose
To construct a simple, working fire extinguisher.

Background
While touring a local fire museum, you and your partner came across an old fire extinguisher. Neither of you had ever seen anything like it. It was torpedo shaped and had a rubber hose attached near the top. There was no trigger, and the instructions on the side said, *"Turn upside down and direct hose toward the base of the fire."*

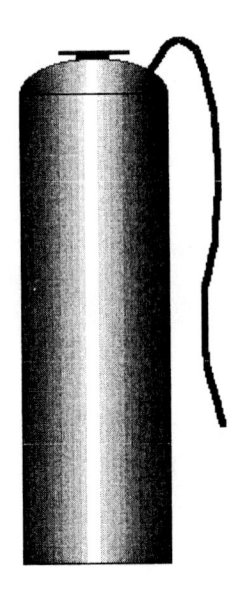

Why would you have to turn the "torpedo" upside down? Why wasn't there a trigger? How could it put out a fire?

The museum curator decided to demonstrate the old relic for you. She flipped the fire extinguisher over while holding the hose away from her. A stream of liquid came shooting out! How?

Materials
For each pair:
- large-mouth glass jar or beaker
- baking soda
- water
- candle
- matches
- goggles
- toothpicks
- tweezers
- vinegar
- 16-oz or 20-oz soda bottle with lid
- hammer
- nail
- facial tissue
- washtub, bucket, or sink
- newspaper

Part A

Procedure
Work with a partner. Put a small amount of baking soda in the bottom of a glass jar or beaker. Add a little water to dissolve the baking soda. Hold a toothpick with tweezers, light it with the candle, and lower it into the jar. Don't let the burning toothpick touch the solution. Observe and record what happens. **Caution:** Wear goggles during all controlled burns.

Now add about a tablespoon of vinegar to the solution. Wait 5 to 10 seconds or until the bubbling stops. Now repeat the burning-toothpick test. Again record your observations.

In your journal, describe the reaction between vinegar and baking soda, and speculate on what chemical the bubbles might be made of.

Part B

Procedure
Poke a hole in the center of the cap of a soda bottle. Add about 2 centimeters of vinegar and 2 centimeters of water to the bottle. Invent a way to use facial tissue to suspend about a teaspoon of dry baking soda in the closed bottle.

Brainstorm a way to quickly mix the baking soda and vinegar without removing the bottle cap. Place your finger tightly over the hole, and don't tip the bottle until you're ready to extinguish a fire.

In a washtub, bucket, or sink, have your partner hold a lit toothpick with tweezers. Use your technique to quickly mix the baking soda with the vinegar-water solution. Slowly and carefully aim the hole in the bottle toward the flame, and then remove your finger.

Answer these questions in your journal:
- Why does the liquid shoot out of your fire extinguisher?
- Why does soda shoot out of an open bottle or can if you drop it?

40   Fire!

Conclusion
Your team has decided to start a business. You will manufacture and market large fire extinguishers made to your specifications.
1. Decide which of the following industries you will target in your ads:
   - the oil industry
   - the paper industry
   - the lumber industry
   - electric companies
2. Write a business letter to a bank asking for a small-business loan to get your company started. Be sure to justify your decision about which industry your company will target.
3. Prepare a colorful brochure about your fire extinguisher. Your brochure must contain these items:
   - a cross-sectional drawing labeled to show how your fire extinguisher works
   - an illustration of the type(s) of fire(s) your fire extinguisher should be used on
   - simple operating instructions

STUDENT VOICES

My area was one of the worst hit by the fires, McKendrie Woods. Almost all of the houses there were burnt, except they saved the model homes. My mom was kinda mad about that.

I wasn't there when we were evacuated. They told my mom to get out of the house. She had to leave right away and only had time to grab a few pictures.

One thing we lost was our cats—three adult cats and a kitten. Earlier, I had tried to get them out but they wouldn't go in the car, and my mom didn't have time to get them when she was evacuated. My mom was in a state of shock or something—she went to the hairdresser! The whole duplex was burnt to the ground. We had to make a list of all of the stuff we lost, and they are going to try to help us on it.

The way fire behaves is unpredictable—it can jump. Most of the grass on the sides of the road were charred, but the rest of it was fine; you can see where the fire jumped. The ashes from the fire help make the ground greener; they fertilize it. Most of the palmetto trees in the area have already grown back.

CHRIS BUTCHER
PALM COAST, FL

On the Job

Veteran Firefighter

Terri Gartenmayer
Trevose Fire Company,
Station No. 4
Trevose, Pennsylvania

Terri Gartenmayer teaches by day and fights fires by night. She's been an official member of the Trevose Fire Company since she was 16. These days, at 26, she is a sixth grade teacher at Maple Point Middle School in Langhorne, Pennsylvania, and works with the Trevose Fire Company, where she was recently voted president—the first woman to hold the job since the all-volunteer company was founded in 1926. Gartenmayer is teaching, working toward her master's degree, and expecting her first child. So while she's not actively putting out fires at the moment, she expects her kids to follow in that tradition, as she happens to be married to a firefighter. So you might say fire fighting is in Terri Gartenmayer's past, present, and future.

My dad was a firefighter, and I grew up going with him to the firehouse when I was younger, along with my brothers. So it was not a surprise for my family when I joined the fire company at 16.

Being a female firefighter is not as bad as you might think. Yes, there are scary moments. You wonder if you have enough air in your airpack and if you have enough water in the line, or if the water will be there when you need it—things like that. In the beginning, I thought it was going to be difficult, being a woman in the company, but as I progressed through the years, I found it wasn't as hard as I thought it would be. It's gotten much better over the years. Men are becoming more accepting of women, but most women still don't realize that they can join this profession. They still think of it as male dominated.

Most of the people in Bucks County, Pennsylvania, are volunteer firefighters. We average 400 calls a year. Some weeks we get no calls, and other times we might get six calls in one day. Some nights we don't get a lot of sleep.

If kids are going to be camping in the woods, they really need to think about the things they are bringing with them, especially if they're flammables.

If you're building a camp, you need to consider location. Does the camp have access to water? You can't have a truck in the woods, so you have to think about how you will get water if a fire starts. If you can't pump the water, you'll have to draft water from a river or lake. And to do that, you'll need to build something that creates suction.

Fire companies sometimes have to draft water, but it isn't easy. You can create something like a septic pump to get the water out of the lake, if you need it, but is very difficult and takes several people.

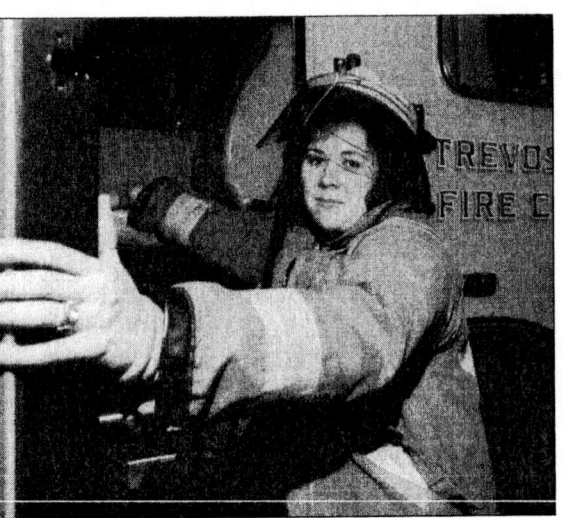

You won't have electricity out in the woods, either, so you might need a supply of gas to power a pump. You have to think about what you'll need ahead of time—and how to get the resources *before* something happens.

If you want to become a firefighter, one way to get experience is just to call the local fire department and volunteer. Here, kids can become junior firefighters when they are 14. They can't ride the trucks, but they can get practice with the equipment. Then if they join the force, they'll be that much further ahead than the other new people. Sometimes we have kids doing volunteer fire fighting for community service through the courts and they end up joining the company.

Before we can start fighting fires, we have to go through extensive training. They don't just hand you a hose and tell you to go out there. We do a lot of hands-on training and drills.

Courtesy Joe Dixon, Bucks County Courier Times

In training, we learn how to use an airpack and hoses. You have to demonstrate that you can use the equipment. For example, you're tested to make sure you can take apart your mask and put it back together. You're tested to see how long it takes you to put your airpack on—you should do this in less than two minutes. You're tested on how to pack and pull hose. These are not book tests, although you need to pass some written exams to become certified by the state.

Some of what we do is dangerous. In our training, we learn how to put out fires in a burning building. We also learned how to rappel down a five- or six-story tower. When I took the ropes and riggings class, I was concerned at first about doing it, but once I did it, I knew I wanted to do this again. You have to learn how to rappel in case you are stuck on a hill or have to rescue and carry a person out of a fire.

Right now I'm pregnant, so I can't go out to the actual fires. Not going is the hardest part for me. I can't just sit when there's a fire, so I go to the station and help out however I can, making sure the firefighters have enough food, or I might handle paperwork for the chief at a fire.

You do use a lot of science on the job, although you probably won't think about it at the time. For instance, you need to understand about pressure so you have the right amount of pressure in your hose for the water.

Sometimes the work is scary, but you get so much adrenaline running in a dangerous situation, you just keep going. This is a team. We all have to work together. You never go out alone; two people always go out together, and two people come back at the same time. We always have backups, just like police.

I was the first female elected president of our company. It was an achievement, but I think maybe it will encourage more women to join. We have six female firefighters in our company right now. Of course you have to prove yourself, but that's true whether you are male or female. If you don't prove yourself, you're not going to be as accepted. People who volunteer for this job do it because they want to help their community. We know we are not getting paid to fight fires, but we all show a lot of pride in our company. It's a job with a lot of camaraderie and satisfaction.

Firefighters silhouetted against the flames of a burning building

Discovery File

Sprinklers, Smoke Detectors, and Fire Extinguishers

Fire-safety technology has produced three main products: automatic sprinklers, smoke detectors, and specialized fire extinguishers.

Sprinkler Systems

Automatic sprinkler systems have been in use since 1874, when American inventor Henry Parmalee created one to protect his piano.

A sprinkler system is a network of pipes leading to multiple sprinkler heads. Various devices hold the water back at the sprinkler head. But when there is a fire, the heat melts a special metal, and pressurized sprays of water or other fire-suppressing chemicals shower down on the flames.

Most sprinklers take about 90 seconds to activate, but the newest models claim to activate in only 14 seconds.

Millions of sprinkler systems can be found in apartment buildings, hospitals, jails, schools, and offices in the United States. To firefighters, sprinkler systems are critical to keeping a fire under control before they arrive on the scene.

Automatic sprinkler systems are the single most effective method of fighting fires in their early stages. A sprinkler can detect and control a fire, and some even sound an alarm.

Without an automatic sprinkler system, a fire in a high-rise building can quickly rage out of control. Buildings over 75 feet high present a special challenge to firefighters and rescue teams whose ladders do not go higher. Unfortunately, building codes requiring sprinkler systems apply only to new housing; many older buildings do not have them in place.

Smoke Detectors

You probably have at least one smoke detector in your home. This device emits a loud warning sound at the first sign of smoke. There are two main kinds of smoke detectors: *photoelectric* (optical) and *ionization*.

In the photoelectric type, smoke interferes with a beam of light, causing a change in the flow of electric current. Ionization alarms are activated when smoke particles attach themselves to *ions* (charged particles) created in the detector by a minute radioactive source, thus reducing the flow of current.

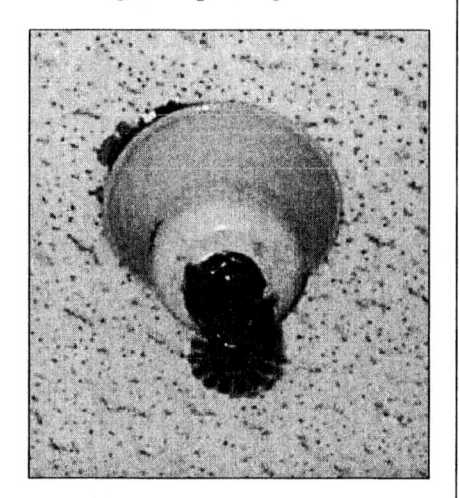

Sprinkler head in a ceiling

Safety experts say that smoke detectors are most effective when they are installed on the ceiling or high on a wall, away from air vents.

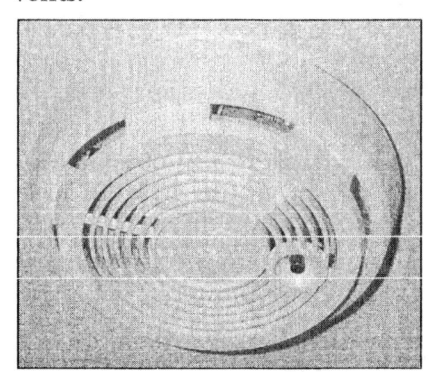

Household smoke detector

Local fire ordinances typically require that smoke detectors be installed in public buildings, homes, and offices, but laws regarding new houses vary. However, firefighters credit smoke detectors and sprinkler systems with reducing death by fires in the United States.

Fire Extinguishers

While you might think water is the first thing you should put on a fire, that is not always the case. Other extinguishing agents work much better than water, depending on the nature of the fire. And some fires are actually made worse by the addition of water.

Early fire extinguishers were just metal cylinders filled with a solution of sodium bicarbonate (baking soda) and water under a container of sulfuric acid. A firefighter turned the cylinder

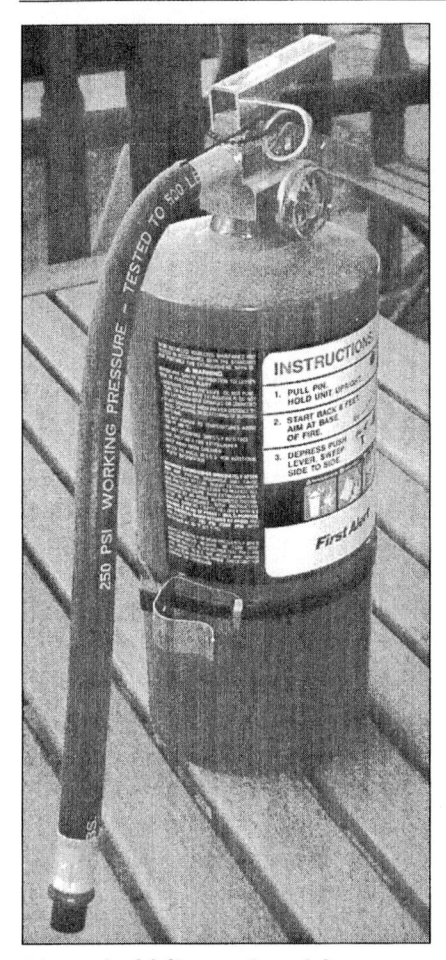

Household fire extinguisher

upside down so the acid mixed with the baking-soda solution to form carbon dioxide gas. The carbon dioxide expanded, and a small, handheld hose was used to spray the liquid on the fire.

Fire-prevention experts classify fires into four groups—A, B, C, and D—depending on the material that is burning. A specific fire extinguisher is available for each type of fire. A multipurpose, dry-chemical extinguisher that works on different kinds of fires is commonly used in homes and other locations where various types of fires might occur.

- **Class A** fires involve ordinary combustible materials like cloth, paper, and wood. Water or water-based liquids will extinguish the fire by cooling the fuel below its kindling point; smothering the fire with dry chemicals also works.

- **Class B** fires involve flammable and combustible liquids like greases, oils, and gasoline. These fires can be extinguished by removing one of the sides of the fire triangle; shutting out the air, for instance. Class B extinguishers use dry chemicals, carbon dioxide, or foam.

- **Class C** fires, which involve electrical equipment, computers, motors, and switches, must be extinguished with an agent that does not conduct electricity. For this purpose, dry chemicals or carbon dioxide is used.

- **Class D** fires involve combustible metals like magnesium and require a smothering, heat-absorbing extinguishing agent that does not react with the burning metal. These fires require special extinguishers for specific metals.

Water extinguishers should be used only on Class A fires. Water conducts electricity and *should never be used* to fight electrical fires (Class C). A multipurpose fire extinguisher that fights fires in Classes A, B, and C is probably in place in your school and your home. A heat reaction between the chemical and the fire creates carbon dioxide, which puts out the fire.

A chemical called *halon* was used to suppress electrical and airplane fires until it was phased out beginning in 1993. It was discovered that halon damaged the atmosphere's protective ozone layer. Scientists have been experimenting with replacement chemicals since halon was removed from use.

Safety Check
It's a good idea to check the fire-safety measures in place in your own home.

- Are smoke alarms installed and operating properly? Batteries need to be changed regularly.

- Are fire extinguishers present, accessible, and of the right type? Does everyone know where they are and how to operate them? The label on a fire extinguisher will tell you what kinds of fires it works on and how to operate it.

- Does your family have an evacuation plan?

Discovery File

Recovery After a Wildfire

Unlike the way they are portrayed in cartoons, animals do not panic and flee a burning forest in a stampeding herd. Larger animals like bears, elk, moose, and deer simply walk away. Bison and elk will even graze on the flaming edges of the fire. Animals that do perish are more likely to be killed by smoke than fire.

Small animals like rodents do run away quickly. They are often caught by larger mammals, such as foxes and coyotes, that take advantage of a fire to chase their prey out of their hiding places.

But what happens after a wildfire burns out or is extinguished?

Even while the ground is still warm from the fire, insects begin busily scuttling and scurrying around doing their thing. Ants, beetles, millipedes, centipedes, and other insects return to the surface. Fire beetles seek out a burned area where they can breed and lay their eggs in charred logs.

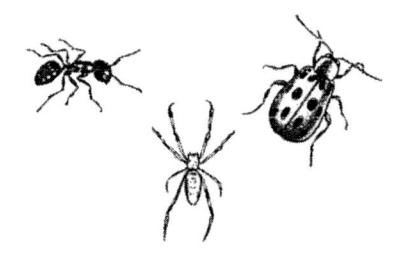

Many birds and mammals have adaptations that enable them to cope with the effects of a wildfire. For example, dead trees provide perfect nesting spots for birds. In fact, the National Park Service keeps a few dead trees for this purpose in each acre of burned woodland. There is even a name for dead trees that are still standing: *snags*.

Lodgepole pine, a tree that grows in the western highlands and makes up most of our western forests, is one of many species adapted to fire. Lodgepole pines produce two kinds of pine cones. The first opens normally and the seeds sprout. The second seals the seeds in pine resin that melts only in the heat of a fire. The fire burns away the resin, allowing the seeds to escape and begin another forest. After the 1988 Yellowstone fires, seed counts from sealed pinecones were high, demonstrating that the cones had indeed opened in the fire. Seeds not eaten by animals sprouted, and seeds eaten by rodents and other small mammals were dispersed to other areas.

As a forest grows, it goes through several stages of development known as *succession*. The first stage of growth after a major fire begins with *pioneer species* like lodgepole pine and aspen. Eventually, a forest will become dominated by other species, such as alpine fir. Over time, an *old-growth* or *climax forest* will completely replace the pioneer species.

In the spring that followed the 1988 fires, Yellowstone enjoyed a bumper crop of wildflowers growing in the burned areas. *Fireweed*, a unique fire species (plants or animals that have adapted to fire), sprang up soon after the fires. Other species, like aster, lupine, and other flowers, were thriving. And less than two years after the fires, the young lodgepole pines that had sprouted from seeds released by the heat of the fires were already waist high.

Even in the Florida Everglades, periodic wildfires help preserve the fragile ecosystem. After a fire there, plants send up new growth that provides food for species like white-tailed deer and wild hogs, which in turn attract and help sustain the endangered Florida panther.

Check with fire experts in your region of the country. Perhaps there are recently burned areas that you can help monitor. But, whether or not you monitor them, they will recover.

46   Fire!

THE STORY—PART 4

Fire in America: The Last 150 Years

The Great Chicago Fire In October 1871, the United States experienced the two worst fires in its history. The most infamous of these fires happened in Chicago and destroyed a large portion of the city. "One dark night, when we were all asleep, old Mrs. O'Leary left the lantern in the barn. And when the cow kicked it over, she winked her eye and said, there'll be a hot time in the old town tonight. Fire! Fire! Fire!"

You may have sung this song around a campfire. But is there any truth to the story it tells? While it's possible that a kerosene lantern could have started the blaze that burned one third of Chicago in 1871, no one knows for sure.

What we do know is that during October 1871, the weather was hot and dry. Only one and a half inches of rain had fallen since July 4. At the time, Chicago was a wooden town. Houses, stores, churches, and many other buildings were made of wood. After all, Chicago was a lumber center.

You might say the Chicago of 1871 was one giant fire hazard. In addition to nearly 600 miles of wooden sidewalks and its fast-burning wooden buildings, Chicago also had paint factories, distilleries, gasworks (manufacturing plants for gas), lumberyards, furniture manufacturers, coal distributors, and small sheds.

Like many cities at the time, Chicago averaged about two reported fires per day. And on the night before the Great Fire, another fire took more than 16 hours to control. On Sunday, October 8, a strong wind blew from the southwest—fanning the first flames of the fire.

A series of fateful errors—including a failure to sound the fire alarm, broken alarm boxes, alarms

The Rush for Life over the Randolph Street Bridge, 1871

sent to the wrong firehouse, plus firefighters tired and drunk after the previous night's fire—allowed the fire to get out of control at a time when it still might have been contained.

The Great Chicago fire burned for more than 24 hours and ended only when the winds died down and rains arrived. Three hundred people died, and over 100,000 were left homeless. Chicago rebuilt and emerged as a major metropolis of the Midwest, but the legend of Mrs. O'Leary's cow lives on.

Mrs. O'Leary lived in one of the shanties in an area that wealthier Chicago residents wanted to have condemned. Anti-immigrant attitudes may have helped place the blame on Catherine and Patrick O'Leary and their cow—the O'Leary's were Irish.

In the summer of 1997, a researcher did what no one had done in more than 100 years: plotted a map of the buildings involved in the fire and traced the fire's route, proving conclusively that the O'Leary's cow could not have started the fire. Apparently, the "eyewitness" reports were less than accurate; houses and a fence would have prevented the main witness from seeing what he claimed to have seen.

The Peshtigo Fires What most people don't know is that on the same night the Great Chicago Fire began, another and even larger fire started in the small town of Peshtigo, Wisconsin. North of Chicago, Peshtigo was the lumber center of the region. Like Chicago, Peshtigo had also experienced a very dry summer. In fact, the whole region was so dry that people's eyes watered from the smoke in the air from small fires that kept starting in the forest.

On the night of October 8, 1871, fires in the forest spread into the town, causing mass panic. People scurried in all directions, trying to escape. People running toward a bridge from one side of the river ran into a crowd of people running from the opposite side. The wooden bridge caught fire, and the people on it drowned. The fire destroyed everything in Peshtigo and would have kept burning if it were not for the rain that began to fall on the afternoon of October 9—the same rain that put out the fire in Chicago. In the Peshtigo fire, about 1200 people died and more than 1.2 million acres of timberland were destroyed.

Nineteenth-century advances The Industrial Revolution led to many innovations in fire-fighting equipment. Wagons went from being pulled by men to being pulled by horses. Then came the steam-powered pumps. And a chemical engine even carried a mixture of baking soda and an acid for fighting small fires. Alarm boxes became commonplace.

Famous fires of the twentieth century Tragically, it would take many more fires to teach more lessons about fire safety and prevention. With each fatal fire came new laws and regulations, too late for the people and property destroyed, but lessons that would benefit future generations.

Triangle Shirtwaist Factory, 1911 This horrific fire, the worst ever in New York's factories, took the lives of many young women and girls and changed history. Until this fire, thousands of workers, many of them children, worked six days a week in New York's *sweatshops.* Fire safety was not a priority for most bosses.

Late in the afternoon of Saturday, March 25, the workers at the Triangle factory were finishing their sewing of shirtwaists, or blouses. At 4:45 P.M., as they were preparing to leave the ten-story building on the city's Lower East Side, someone noticed a fire smoldering in a rag bin on the eighth floor. Flames quickly spread to the paper and cloth scraps covering the wooden tables and floors.

Within minutes, the eighth floor was on fire. Workers ran toward the exit, only to find the doors bolted from the outside (so managers could prevent anyone from sneaking out for a break). The fire spread to the ninth floor. Desperate workers jumped from windows and into elevator shafts, where they fell to their deaths. The intense heat softened the building's single fire escape, making it useless. Firefighters' ladders reached only to the sixth floor. In minutes, 146 employees were dead or dying.

In the investigation that followed, it was determined that many laws had been broken. Sprinkler systems had not been installed. Exit doors were locked. This disaster again led to new and stronger fire codes for New York and other large cities.

Coconut Grove, 1942 On the night of November 28, 1942, after an exciting football game, more than 1000 people crowded into this Boston nightclub, built to hold about half that many patrons. It was wartime, and people were eager for a night out. Late that night, a small fire broke out in the club; waiters tried to put it out with seltzer bottles and wet towels, but the fire grew. People panicked and tried to escape but, trapped in the darkness and smoke, they were unable to find a way out. One exit door had been welded shut, and the doors that did work opened inward. As people pressed against them to escape, a human wall sealed the exits.

The fire moved quickly. *Nitrous oxide* produced by burning plastics acted as an anesthetic, causing some people to pass out and die from smoke inhalation. In all, 492 people died.

Once again, it took a disaster to underscore the need for fire exits and laws about the number of people allowed to be in a public building at one time.

Twentieth-century technology Eventually, the internal combustion engine replaced the horse. By the 1920s, the horse-drawn fire wagons were gone, and shiny motorized fire engines took their place.

Technology has provided us with sprinklers, smoke detectors, and fire-resistant materials for buildings and furnishings. And yet, the deadliest fires today are often made worse by toxic chemicals from these same materials.

IN THE NEWS

Fire chars timber town's future

Damage toll mounting in the West

By Bob Twigg
USA TODAY

FOSSIL, Ore. — Mike Medlock is waiting for salvage loggers to clear the charred remains of a family legacy.

The retired construction equipment driver had intended to leave his four grandchildren and seven great-grandchildren a 300-acre stand of prime pine trees growing on the 1,120-acre ranch where he grew up.

Medlock, 75, had nurtured the timber, keeping it thin and clean, "since I was big enough to start to work."

Then wildfire swept through. All that's left now is fodder for salvagers. "It all went," he says, sighing.

His story and worse is being repeated across the West as fire turns nearly 500,000 acres into blackened moonscapes.

In the Southwest, a long drought made the land a tinderbox. To the north, a wet winter and spring fed the high grass and forest; but the summer has been hot and dry, and thunderstorms have brought more fire-starting lightning than rain. Put it all together, and you have the ingredients for wildfires spread out from Washington state to Texas.

"It won't be over till it rains ... more than a shower," says Rene Snyder at the Interagency Fire Center in Boise, Idaho.

That means the smoky haze over places like Fossil, a community of 430 people in the foothills of the Cascade Range, won't blow away soon.

Fossil is the government seat of Wheeler County. The 1,713-square-mile county is larger than Rhode Island, but home to just 1,400 people.

Fires are a part of life here.

Near Roseburg, Ore.: Firefighter Alisa Resch douses hot spots in a 12-acre fire in the Umpqua National Forest.

One day two weeks ago, lightning sparked 25 separate blazes that damaged less than 10 acres. But big fires, like the one finally doused over the weekend, are rare.

It started on Aug. 8. Winds of up to 80 mph swept flames over thousands of acres of timber and grassland, 14 houses, five vacation cabins and countless outbuildings. The loss in buildings alone is estimated at $3 million.

Mike VanDeHey lost both the 6,000-square-foot brick and frame mansion he was building and a mobile home.

VanDeHey, 56, started the dream house in 1981. He was almost finished with the exterior, which included a "fireproof" tile roof.

Still, he is not without hope: "Things will get green again."

Down the road, Rockey and Rahlie Goodell and their neighbor Bob Neary echo that halfhearted optimism.

The fire rolled over three-fourths of the Goodells' 5,000-acre Corncob Farm. They raise cattle and horses and run a small "dude ranch."

"We'll start with fixing the fences," says Rockey Goodell. "Cattle are running all over."

The Goodells expect to be able to feed their cattle with hay from some land outside the fire zone.

"That means I can't sell it and can't make my (farm debt) payments," says Rockey. Will they lose the farm? Rahlie shakes her head no.

Talk of prices — especially timber and hay — pepper every conversation around here.

The most repeated question: Will burned timber bring a decent price?

The timber market is depressed right now, says Wheeler County assessor Don Cossitt, a former contract logger. All that salvage timber will deflate prices even more.

That's bad news for the county, already strained by the loss of revenue from logging on federal land.

Last year, the government paid the county $1.6 million in fees. This year, with little logging on federal lands, the county expects only $250,000.

The county also will collect less in fees from logging of burned timber, while facing higher costs for the sheriff's and roads departments because of the fire.

"We're barely surviving now," says Jeanne Burch, a county commissioner and Fossil city administrator.

County voters will decide in November whether to approve a tax increase. Until then, Burch is pushing for state disaster relief while awaiting word on federal aid.

47 wildfires in 8 states worsen historic season

Firefighters battled 47 blazes in eight states Sunday as one of the nation's worst wildfire seasons continued.

Nearly 500,000 acres are burning, including the Simnasho fire in Oregon, where 109,000 acres of grass, brush and timber are afire.

The fire swept across the Warm Springs Indian Reservation last week, destroying 10 homes and forcing the evacuation of 200 people. By Sunday, the fire was 70% contained.

The reservation is about 90 miles southeast of Portland.

Cooler conditions may help firefighters contain all of the fire by Tuesday.

Fires also are burning in California, Colorado, Montana, Idaho, Wyoming, Utah and Nevada. Control of the 15,160-acre Adelaide Complex of fires in the Fishlake National Forest in Utah was expected Sunday night.

Since Jan. 1, 4.1 million acres have burned. That many acres have not burned this early in the season in the past 30 years, says Janelle Smith of the Interagency Fire Center in Boise, Idaho.

By Carol J. Castaneda

The Story—Part 4

DISCOVERY FILE

Food Keeps Your "Fire" Burning

You're hungry, so you stop at the snack bar. You read the nutrition labels on your favorite foods. A candy bar has 200 calories; a bag of chips, 300; a soda, 150; a package of chocolate chip cookies, 400. What do these numbers mean?

You've heard that food is fuel, but what does that mean?

Like gasoline for your car and wood for a campfire, food is a fuel for your body—its cells, blood vessels, muscles, nerves, and all its other components. You're obviously not on fire in the same way, but *respiration* is very similar to combustion, only it happens in your body, and it happens more slowly.

Respiration is the process of using oxygen to break down food. Fire is the process of using oxygen to break down fuel. In that way, respiration and fire are similar. But fire gives off heat, light, carbon dioxide, and sound as its byproducts. Respiration—a chemical reaction that occurs in the *mitochondria* within every cell in your body—gives off heat, carbon dioxide, and ATP (adenosine triphosphate, a high-energy molecule that your cells use to power their activities).

When your body is working on that bag of chips or package of cookies, it is literally "burning" calories. When calories are burned, energy is released. How does this process work?

For starters, when you breathe in oxygen, it passes from your lungs into the *hemoglobin* molecules of your red blood cells. The oxygen combines with the hemoglobin, turning the blood a bright red. When oxygenated blood passes near busy muscle cells, the oxygen detaches from the hemoglobin molecules and passes out of the blood and into the muscles. Inside the mitochondria, within the muscle cells, the oxygen reacts with food molecules the same way oxygen does when something burns, producing CO_2 and the energy the body requires (ATP).

When substances react with oxygen, they are said to be *oxidized*. By oxidizing certain compounds, your body produces energy. You eat food, which is then "burned," or oxidized. Without the energy you get from food, your body would not be able to function.

Calories Aren't Always Bad

When food is "burned" in any animal's body, the chemical energy stored in the food is released. Different foods release different amounts of energy. The energy is measured in Calories or kilocalories or a newer unit, the kilojoule (kJ); 1 Calorie = 4.187 kJ.

A calorie is so small a unit that when we say "calorie" we almost always are talking about a kilocalorie, or a unit of 1000 calories. One kilocalorie (kcal) is the amount of heat energy required to raise the temperature of 1000 grams of water 1 degree Celsius. The food Calorie (note the capital C) people talk about so much is really a kilocalorie. So the bag of chips you just ate contains 300 food Calories, or 300 kilocalories.

Your body requires a certain number of calories just to exist, even if you are doing "nothing"—your body needs fuel to breathe and perform all its other resting functions. If you are more active, you need more fuel—more calories. If you are a less active, couch-potato type, your calorie requirement is going to be less than the jock who plays basketball or ice skates several hours a day.

Even your brain cells need energy to read these lines and process the information.

So how do scientists measure how many calories are in a candy bar?

Scientists called *calorimetrists* measure the caloric content of various foods by burning them

---

Fire
Fuel + Oxygen → Energy + Carbon Dioxide + Water

Respiration
Food + Oxygen → Energy (Heat and ATP) + Carbon Dioxide + Water

in chambers called *combustion calorimeters*. The calorimeter shows how much heat energy is produced by different foods. The food to be tested is placed into one of these enclosed chambers, and the chamber is placed inside another container that is filled with water. The food is ignited and allowed to burn completely. As it burns, the food releases energy to warm the water surrounding the chamber. The number of calories released can be calculated from the increase in the temperature of the water.

For example, if 10 peanuts burned in a calorimeter increased the temperature of 1000 grams of water by 40°C, then the average calorie content of one peanut is 4000 calories, or 4 kcal (4 food Calories).

Another way food scientists determine caloric value, or heat energy, of a food is by measuring how much protein, fat, and carbohydrate are contained in the food, because they know that 1 gram of fat contains 9 Calories, while 1 gram of either protein or carbohydrate contains only 4 Calories.

What we also know is that if we don't burn as many calories as we consume, the excess will be stored. Excess fats are stored as fat, while excess carbohydrates are first converted to fats in the liver before they are stored. Storing fat was a good idea for survival back when our ancestors roamed the African savannas and weren't sure when they would find something to eat. But in most industrially advanced countries today, people have an ample supply of food.

Calories alone don't tell the whole story. What if you knew that your daily requirement was about 2000 calories and you decided to get your total calories from either shredded lettuce or chocolate chips? First of all, you would have to consume a great deal of lettuce to obtain 2000 calories. Second, neither food would provide the vitamins and minerals necessary to support the growth and proper function of your body.

IN THE NEWS

Utah blaze threatens major power station

Lightning and gusty winds today could hamper fire crews in Utah, where a 2,900-acre blaze has threatened a major electrical substation and twin 345,000-volt power lines feeding the Las Vegas and Los Angeles areas.

Officials hope to contain the Long Ridge fire near Mona, 65 miles south of Salt Lake City, by late today, but 40-mph wind gusts could push the blaze over fire lines. Flames came within a half-mile of the power substation and its transmission lines, but the fire receded Sunday.

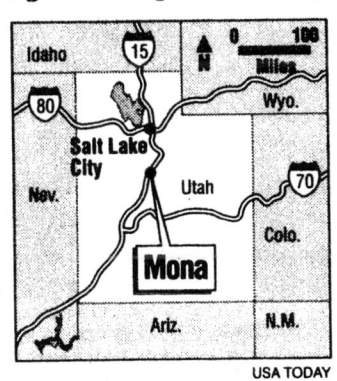

Firefighters also battled blazes, many started by lightning, that had blackened more than 13,500 acres on the New Mexico-Colorado border, nearly 7,000 acres in south New Mexico, more than 2,500 acres in Yakima County, Wash., 1,800 acres in the Boundary Waters Canoe Area near Lutsen, Minn., 660 acres in Swan Quarter National Wildlife Refuge, N.C., and 360 acres near Cajon Pass, Calif.

USA TODAY, 17 JUNE 1996

The Story—Part 4

Fire ravages a home

STUDENT VOICES

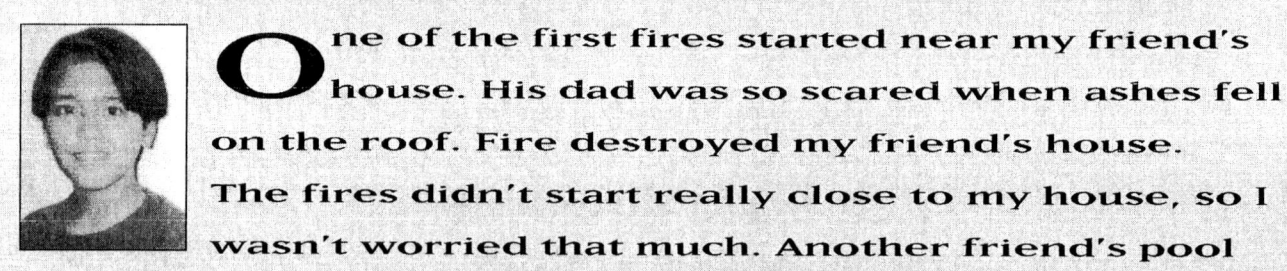

One of the first fires started near my friend's house. His dad was so scared when ashes fell on the roof. Fire destroyed my friend's house. The fires didn't start really close to my house, so I wasn't worried that much. Another friend's pool was full of ashes and other debris. Now there are green leaves growing on the branches and little plants growing on the ground.

Being evacuated was an adventure. I felt scared and excited at the same time. My dad put his lawnmower in his car because he wanted to save it, and we piled our clothes in the car. I traveled to Daytona and around Flagler and it was smelly. The smoke was so foggy that I couldn't see, and it hurt my lungs.

I saw that fires travel on the trees and spread very fast. They can start with just a spark if it is really dry. If a fire is headed your way, don't panic, and remember to take your stuff.

CZAR DEREQUITO
PALM COAST, FL

DISCOVERY FILE

Energy 101

While you are reading these words, you are using many forms of energy. Your body is using energy from food to stay alive and to keep your brain cells energized. The light bulbs in your classroom are using electricity. Your arm muscles are using energy to take notes. Your school is heated or cooled by some form of energy.

Geothermal energy is energy from within our Earth. *Nuclear energy* is the energy stored in the nucleus of such radioactive elements as uranium. Nearly all other forms of energy begin with the sun.

Here on Earth, energy constantly streams toward us from our star—called the sun—93 million miles away. When sunlight reaches the leaves of plants, *photosynthesis* occurs. Through photosynthesis, a plant captures the sun's energy and uses it to build large molecules called *carbohydrates*. Plants are *autotrophs,* which means they make their own food directly from the energy they get from the sun. People, animals, bacteria, and fungi are *heterotrophs*. We get our energy indirectly from the sun by feeding on other plants or animals, and then oxidizing the energy-containing compounds in them.

In a continuous flow, energy arrives from the sun, passes from plant to animal, and then from animal to animal, and then from animal to soil. When undigested waste or a dead animal or plant decays, the energy is used by *decomposer* organisms in the soil. When waste and dead matter do not decompose, they still contain their load of energy.

The energy stored in fossil fuels like coal, oil, and gasoline also came from the sun in this way. These fuels must be burned to finally release their energy—energy that has been stored for millions of years but that can be traced back to sunlight captured by the plants and creatures millions of years ago.

Energy from a burning fossil fuel can be converted into many other forms of energy. If the heat is used to boil water and create steam, the steam can drive a generator, which turns the energy into electrical energy. Electrical energy can then be turned into sound energy, light energy, or radio energy.

Energy is constantly flowing, changing from one form to another, from *potential* or stored energy, into another form and then ultimately back into potential energy. Energy cannot be created or destroyed, but before it can do its work, it must be harnessed to convert it from one form to another. One challenge of the future will be to find energy sources that are clean, safe, and renewable.

Discovery File

The Greenhouse Effect

The *greenhouse effect* is in the news almost daily. Some people believe that it is producing a *global warming*, and that we—the people of the industrialized world—are causing it.

What is the greenhouse effect, are we contributing to it, and what does this have to do with fire?

If you can answer these questions, you probably don't need to read this Discovery File. If you're not sure, or want to know the latest on the issue, keep reading.

The greenhouse effect gets its name from what happens when visible light from the sun hits the plants, soil, and other objects inside a greenhouse. When this happens, some of the visible light is absorbed by the plants and other objects, but some of it is converted into the longer wavelengths of radiation knows as *infrared energy*—another name for heat.

The energy that so easily passed through the windows as visible light cannot totally escape as infrared (heat) energy. Some of the heat is reflected by the glass back toward the plants and soil. As the day goes on, heat builds up and the greenhouse grows warmer.

Earth's atmosphere is like the glass of a greenhouse. The atmosphere lets visible light pass through to the surface but it keeps some of the infrared energy, or heat, from escaping.

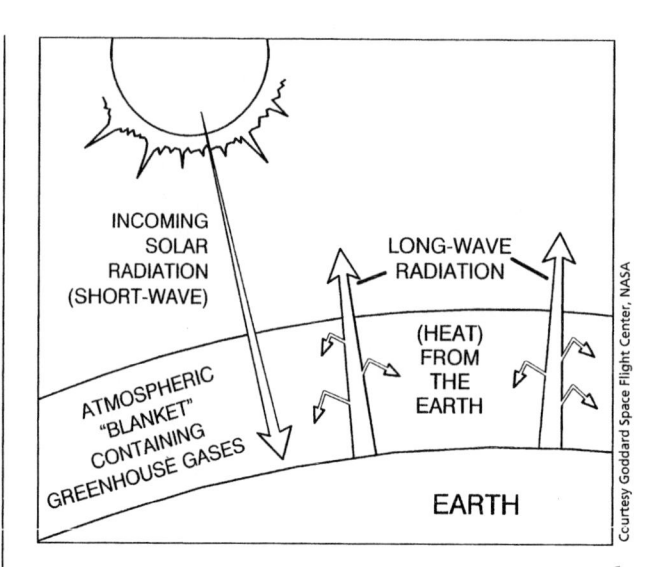

This is actually a good thing! If there were no greenhouse effect, Earth would not be warm enough to support life as we know it. But too much, and Earth may grow too warm. Some people think this is happening now. They believe that Earth's climate is in a warming phase caused by human release of *greenhouse gases* into the atmosphere (greenhouse gases are those that trap heat).

Why do people think this? What is the evidence for a human cause of global warming?

For one thing, the climate is getting warmer. Over the last 150 years, Earth has warmed by about 1.5°C. During that same time, the human population has grown and the release into the atmosphere of greenhouse gases has increased.

Carbon dioxide, methane, nitrogen oxides, and water vapor are four of the greenhouse gases. And, over the last 150 years, as Earth has grown warmer, there has been a steady rise in the amount of carbon dioxide (and other greenhouse gases) in the atmosphere.

Take a look at the graph below. Notice that the level of carbon dioxide in the atmosphere

Atmospheric Carbon Dioxide

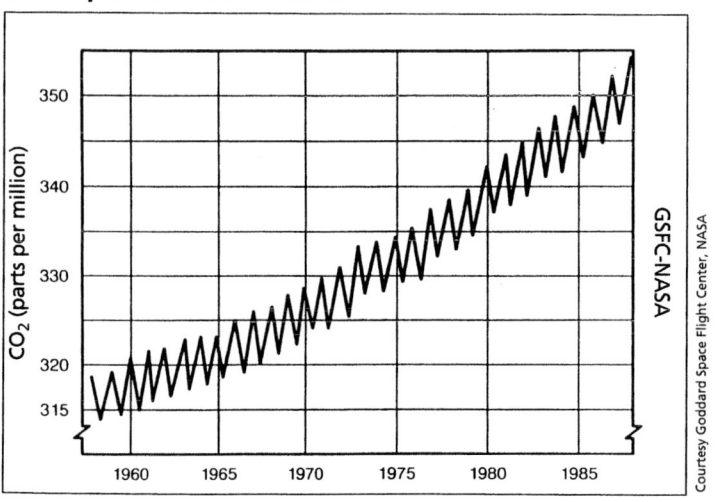

54   Fire!

rises and falls during each calendar year, and that it reaches its highest point in about December and its lowest point in about June. This is easy to explain. First, plants release oxygen into the atmosphere—and absorb carbon dioxide—primarily when their leaves are green or they are actively growing. Second, there is much more land surface in the Northern Hemisphere than the Southern Hemisphere. Thus, when the region where plants are removing the most carbon dioxide from the atmosphere shifts from the Southern Hemisphere to the Northern Hemisphere (which happens during the Northern Hemisphere's spring and summer), the amount of carbon dioxide in the atmosphere falls.

This is where fire comes in: much of the CO_2 being added to the atmosphere comes from fires. As a tree burns, carbon dioxide is released into the atmosphere. (Carbon dioxide also comes from living things as they break down their food, and from volcanic eruptions.)

The Warming Controversy

Whether or not Earth is warming depends on where you start counting. If the starting point for temperature measurement is the sixteenth century, then global temperatures today are lower, not higher. To claim a global warming, it is necessary to begin counting in the middle of the nineteenth century—a time when the so-called "mini–ice age" was ending in many parts of the world.

Evidence suggests that there has been some warming of Earth in recent decades. The temperature record shows it, and the recession of many of Earth's smaller glaciers is further evidence. However, many computer climate models have predicted a greater warming than has actually been observed.

In addition, whether there has been a recent warming of Earth depends on whether you are talking about the surface or the atmosphere. According to the National Climate Data Center, the surface appears to have warmed about 1.0°F (0.55°C) over the last 100 years, with land temperatures warming at a somewhat faster rate than sea-surface temperatures. On the other hand, the same government organization reports that the atmosphere is cooling. In fact, the lower stratosphere (13 to 19 kilometers above the surface of our planet) cooled about 1°C from 1979 to 1999, based on 19 years of satellite observations. Note that the atmospheric-cooling rate is 10 times faster than the surface-warming rate.

If you listen to the news, you probably think we are heading for disaster. However, there is also evidence that a rise in the level of atmospheric carbon dioxide is good for plants. It may actually increase food production. We just don't know all of the ramifications of global warming yet.

We do know that neither the carbon dioxide level nor Earth's climate remains constant for very long. To the contrary, Earth's geologic and human histories have recorded these changes. Global warmings have been followed by global coolings. Ice ages are followed by glacier retreat.

The only thing we know for sure about the current warming trend is that it coincides with a rise in the carbon dioxide level in the atmosphere. We do not yet know that one has *caused* the other. Nor do we know for sure whether human activity is contributing to the warming, but evidence suggests that it has already, or will in the future.

ON THE JOB

Fire Inspector

**RANDY HOLMES
SANTA FE FIRE
DEPARTMENT
SANTA FE, NEW MEXICO**

I've been with the department eight years, the first five as a firefighter and the last three as an inspector. When I was a firefighter, I'd work 24 hours on, then 24 off, for three shifts. After the third shift, I'd be off for four days. As an inspector, I work from 8 to 5, but I'm on call 24 hours a day for a week at a time.

For me, being a fire inspector is like being an archeologist. I go back to the scene minutes, hours, or even days after the fire. I dig through what's left as I try to find evidence indicating whether a fire was accidental or intentional.

Becoming an inspector requires intense training. We learn that evidence from a fire never leaves—it just takes a different shape.

We learn what to look for. We learn how evidence from a fire tells a story and points to where the fire started. There are indicators inside a structure; for example, glass lightbulbs melt toward the side of the heat. Melted glass or plastic can be an indicator pointing directly where the heat source was located. It's one way we determine the area of origin. Then we look for the point of origin to determine exactly where the fire started. Sometimes we can do that, sometimes we can't.

In arson classes, instructors will set different kinds of fires, and our job is to determine the cause. Lately I've been learning about *incendiary devices* like homemade bombs. We have to know what's out there. It's getting a lot tougher for us now; it's very easy for anyone to build a device.

In training for fighting structure fires, we learn building construction, so when we go into a fire, we have an idea of what a building can and can't do. We also learn about *accelerant patterns,* the burn patterns left by a substance like gasoline. People think if they use gas, nobody can see it, but it leaves a pattern.

We're called out while a fire is in progress. We go to the scene and wait until it is secure and safe. We start with the exterior. We look for things like flame patterns out the windows or doors, broken glass, and where the fire vented. Then we begin our interior investigation. We also collect weather reports and other information.

The best place to start is the area with the least fire damage and work our way toward the area of most damage. We photograph everything with video, 35 mm, and Polaroid cameras. We first shoot an overview of a room and then specific areas. Before we move anything, we photograph it. We call this a *layer search.*

Before assuming a fire is intentional, we first rule out anything accidental like electrical possibilities, cigarettes, fireplaces, or kids playing with matches. It might take a while if we have to send out any evidence, like electronic devices, to labs.

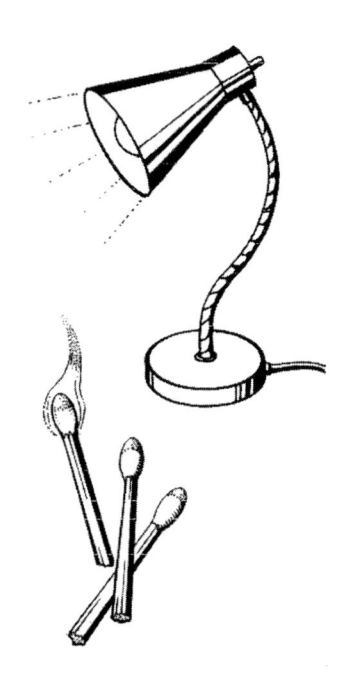

If I can't find anything that will lead me in the direction of an accident, I start looking for evidence of arson. Arson is done for insurance, violence, or crimes

56   Fire!

of passion, and vanity crimes (a person wants to be a hero, sets the fire, and then gets recognition for alerting the fire department).

I didn't start training until I was 30. I did all kinds of things before then. I was a meat cutter and a welder, but I always had a love for the fire department. I lost a brother 8 years ago in an auto accident. Something about that made me feel like I wanted to be out there and make sure if I responded to a call, people would be assured someone cared. I tested for the fire department and started training.

And I love fighting fire. It is dangerous, but great firefighters respect fire and won't put themselves or a partner in danger. We always think about ourselves and our safety before saving a structure.

In Santa Fe, firefighters also handle medical calls. All firefighters must be trained as paramedics or emergency medical technicians (EMT). We don't have private ambulances here, so many of our calls are medical ones.

We don't have high-rise buildings in Santa Fe, but we do have adobe houses. Those are really tough. If we had to ventilate through the ceiling, that would be pretty simple to do in a house, but in some old adobe houses, there's a foot of adobe to cut through.

We experience extreme heat in the summer, so fighting in firegear gets pretty rough. In winter, we experience extreme cold, and water freezes in the lines. Fireplaces are used as source of heat here, so we have a lot more of these fires. People forget to clean them out.

Flames travel from a pan to a stove

Creosote builds up; fire ignites in the chimney, gets into the roof, and causes a house fire. Or they install a wood stove and don't pay attention to safety codes. We have a lot of mobile homes here, which is another problem. A mobile home can go up in 15 minutes. We tell the owners they need to put in smoke detectors.

We've made a big push here for education. We have Fire Prevention Month. We demonstrate how to determine what type of fire extinguisher is appropriate and how to use it. We go to people's houses and help them install smoke detectors. We also help them draw up emergency escape plans. We use the Internet to talk to other firefighters and investigators.

I chose this as my career and I'm very happy with my choice. I think it's the greatest job in the world. I can't think of doing anything else.

The Story—Part 4   57

Discovery File

Is the Sun on Fire?

If we could look deep into the heart of the sun, we would see a "fire." But the sun's fire isn't a real fire. It lacks two of the three components needed by fires here on Earth. The sun's fire has plenty of heat, but it lacks a traditional fuel, and there is no oxygen.

The sun's fire is actually a *nuclear fusion* reaction that has been burning for about 4.7 billion years. Fusion fires on the sun (and other stars) happen when hydrogen, or other lightweight elements, are fused—joined together—into heavier elements. As fusion takes place, energy is released. The energy is in the form of heat and light, just like a real fire. But there is no smoke, soot, or ash left behind. The product of the sun's fire is helium.

When fusion occurs, mass is lost and energy is created. Every minute, the sun converts 240 million tons of its mass into energy. Every minute, Earth receives energy from the sun equal to the amount that would be released from burning thousands of tons of coal.

The temperature at the core of the sun is about 15,000,000 Kelvin, or 27 million degrees Fahrenheit. The temperature in the center is so hot that hydrogen nuclei overcome the force that normally keeps them apart from each other. At these temperatures hydrogen nuclei move so fast that they eventually collide. The collision produces a helium nucleus—two neutrons and two protons—plus a free neutron.

It takes about 1 million years for the heat and light generated by these fusion reactions in the sun's core to travel to the surface of the sun. On the surface it is much cooler—6000 Kelvin, or 10,000 degrees Fahrenheit.

If human beings could reproduce the same fusion fires for use here on Earth, we might not have to worry about running out of fossil fuels. But so far, no one has been able to produce a self-sustaining fusion reaction in the laboratory.

We have, however, made progress toward capturing some of the sun's energy. Harvesting that energy will also reduce the quantity of greenhouse gases that are added to our atmosphere. The push is on to develop alternative sources of energy, and the future for solar power looks bright.

Scientists tell us that a star the size of ours can go on creating helium and giving off energy for about 10 billion years. If they're right, our sun is about halfway through its lifetime.

Whether that time line is right or not, the sun will eventually burn out. And when it does, it will swell to become a *red giant*, then shrink into a *white dwarf*, and Earth will cease to exist!

SCIENCE ACTIVITY

All Fired Up

Purpose
To test some of the variables that influence the spread of forest fires.

Background
With just the right amounts of fuel, heat, and oxygen, a fire can occur.

Forest fires are no different. They may have different causes and they can have different burn patterns, but all forest fires need the same three ingredients as all other fires. However, variations among these and other variables mean that forest fires can end almost as quickly as they start, or they can burn for days or weeks.

The best place to build a camp within a forest may be determined by the way forest fires burn. You and your team members decide to test some of the conditions found on the property to see whether some are more conducive to the spread of fire than others.

Materials
For each team:
- sand
- heatproof-glass or metal pan
- box of toothpicks
- tweezers
- several sheets of paper
- metric ruler
- candle
- matches
- beaker
- sifter or screen
- plastic bag
- goggles

Procedure
Brainstorm with your class the various causes of forest fires and the things in a forest that will burn during a fire. Keep a master list on the chalkboard or on chart paper.

Next, brainstorm with your team some ways you can use the materials available to you to simulate the causes of forest fires that you listed. Toothpicks and paper should be used to simulate trees.

Caution: The total amount of paper used for "treetops" and branches must not be more than a 4-centimeter square. Also, do not use more than 30 "trees" at one time. Wear goggles during all controlled burns.

Spread a layer of sand in a heatproof-glass or metal pan. Keep a lit candle at your station to use for starting simulated forest fires. Put sand in the beaker; you will use it to collect used matches and toothpicks. For safety, when you are building your forests, leave at least a 2-centimeter gap between the forest and the edge of the pan. And never turn your back on the candle!

Hold a lit toothpick with tweezers to start each simulated forest fire. Only start a fire at one spot in the "forest." Record the type of fire you are simulating—such as a lightning strike—where it starts, how it spreads, and what the results are. Draw before-and-after maps of your forest for each test. At the end of each simulation, when the burning has stopped, cover all burnt materials with sand.

Wait several minutes before sifting the waste and ashes from the sand. Pour the waste into the beaker and the sand back into the pan for the next test. Try as many different scenarios as you can in the time your teacher gives you.

Now measure and mark off a 10-centimeter square in the sand. This will be your test area. Repeat the above experiment, again using no more than 30 toothpicks, but this time your "forest" must have a canopy. And it must be designed in such a way that only half the trees catch fire and burn. Try different plans until one works. Draw a map that shows how you accomplished the goal.

Conclusion
You have been asked by the U.S. Forest Service to select a new forest-fire mascot. In addition, you must write a script for a public-service television or radio spot about forest-fire prevention to broadcast across the country.

In your announcement, introduce the new mascot, and use what you have learned from this activity to demonstrate how fires begin and how they spread. Also give people ideas about how they can help prevent forest fires.

IN THE NEWS

Answering the call of the wildfire

The Geronimo Hotshots are among the nation's firefighting elite, although they nearly were disbanded less than two years ago. The 20 American Indians, designated a 'nationally available resource,' spend their summers moving from one hot spot to another.

By Martin Kasindorf
USA TODAY

BENSON, Ariz. — On the rocky slopes of Wrong Mountain, the Geronimo Hotshots are in the final stages of saving Pete Colton's ranch home from flames.

"That'll be it with the bucket for now," fire-crew Superintendent Mike Longknife radios a helicopter dropping 500-gallon buckets of water on a fire in Coronado National Forest.

After two days on the rattlesnake-infested mountain, Longknife's "hotshot" firefighters are declaring the lightning-sparked fire contained. Though small, the blaze had threatened ranches, the Western movie set where Kurt Russell starred in *Tombstone* and the cactuses of Saguaro National Monument. By the time it's out, the fire has burned only 150 acres of mountain brush. All structures are untouched.

"You guys were in there just right," the helicopter pilot tells Longknife. "You really did a good job. Thank you."

For the 20 American Indians who wear the red hard hats of the elite Geronimo Hotshots, the praise is routine. So is the 100-degree desert heat. Likewise, the emergency dispatch orders that last month forced Longknife, 31, to skip his son Orien's first birthday on the San Carlos Apache reservation three hours to the north.

"I miss out on a lot of stuff like this," Longknife says.

It's another summer fire season, a time of little rest for the 53 hotshot teams operating under the Bureau of Indian Affairs, National Park Service, U.S. Forest Service and Bureau of Land Management.

They're the best of the best, these firefighters who lead the U.S. government's 15,000-member fire protection forces. Designated as "nationally available resources," they spend the summer roving from one fire to the next, their movements directed by the National Interagency Fire Center in Boise, Idaho. Only after they undergo 80 hours of fire-suppression training and tough jogging regimens each year can hotshots earn the name.

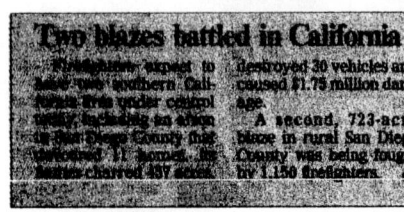

Two blazes battled in California

Firefighters expect to have two southern California fires under control today, including fire which in San Diego County that destroyed 17 homes, 66 homes, charred 437 acres, destroyed 30 vehicles and caused $1.75 million damage.

A second, 723-acre blaze in rural San Diego County was being fought by 1,150 firefighters.

On as little as 30 minutes of notice, Longknife's crew leaves its 1.8-million acre reservation to "eat smoke" in high ponderosa forest, steep brush or windy grassland. While lesser-ranked "Type 2" crews mind fires at home, hotshots see the nation.

They're the crack infantry troops in this paramilitary fire work in the wild. "We get involved when a fire looks like it's going to be long-term and they need some ground-pounders that will get out and do the job," Longknife says.

He and his hotshots drive up to 1,000 miles on fire calls in two "crew buggies," 10-seat trucks littered with equipment, maps and books. They drape 40 pounds of chainsaws, radios and specialty tools, and as many as six water canteens, on their suits of flame-resistant Nomex. They're sent in by foot or helicopter on "initial attack" or as reinforcements. And they're self-sufficient for 24 hours without resupply.

Longknife's job is to assess terrain and winds, decide on a frontal or indirect assault and deploy his troops. Hotshots direct water and retardant drops from aerial tankers. They use saws and dig-and-chop tools to clear brush and vegetation around a fire to starve it of fuel.

If winds pick up and the fire makes a sudden run at them, hotshots use flares to start backfires that scorch the ground and likewise rob the fire of fuel.

Hazards include boulders and flaming weeds that can roll downhill on firefighters in seconds. And bears have been known to steal food supplies.

Hotshots have been moaning about a slow start this year. Rare early rains soaked the mountainous West, leaving southern California the only area in clear and continuing danger.

From Jan. 1 through July 31, only 40,867 fires had burned 2,177,099 acres. In the same period in 1996, 77,608 fires burned 3,254,494 acres, the Boise fire center says. Last year's fire season was especially devastating, with 96,363 blazes charring more than 6 million acres in all.

Despite the slow start, the Geronimo Hotshots have found enough to keep them occupied. Already they have labored this year in Arizona, California and New Mexico.

But the Geronimo Hotshots haven't always been as highly regarded as they are today.

The team was upgraded to hotshot status in 1991 and named itself for the 19th century Chiricahua Apache warrior-chieftain. But by March 1996, the Geronimo team was an undisciplined crew in deep trouble. "They were going to disband it," Longknife says.

Team members cited problems with alcohol abuse, nepotism and a know-it-all attitude. Fire calls were missed when members couldn't be found.

To save the program, the tribe turned to a non-Apache. Longknife, a Gros Ventre tribal member from Hayes, Mont., was living on the San Carlos reservation with his Apache wife, Dina. On the strength of 10 years' hotshot experience in Helena, Mont., and Globe, Ariz., he rebuilt the team.

Longknife's rules: Random drug tests, high-altitude runs, weightlifting and no alcohol on or off duty.

"The ultimate objective of this is their safety," he says.

Hot on fire's trail: On as little as 30 minutes of notice, the Geronimo Hotshots, left, led by Mike Longknife, foreground, can leave their Arizona reservation to fight fires in high ponderosa forest, steep brush or windy grassland, across the nation. Hotshot Charles Hooke, above, works on his chainsaw after battling a blaze near Benson, Ariz.

Photos by Mary Chind for USA TODAY

60   Fire!

STUDENT VOICES

The fires that hit my area were horrible. It was like a bad dream I couldn't wake up from. Fire was everywhere, and smoke was all around us. On the news they said the fire was going 30 miles per hour. It spread all over the place.

Our whole county was told to leave. I didn't know what to take; I was scared and confused. My brother, my dog, and my cat—we all got out.

Before they reopened our county, my mom and I were at her job watching TV. We didn't think our house had burnt down at that point because we had called the police number and they said it was okay. Then we saw my house on the TV, and Mom started crying. She didn't know if we had any insurance.

There's green stuff growing in the woods now, and it doesn't look as bad as it did. They are cutting down the dead trees to make it look better and to help stop this from happening again, and plowing down the houses and putting up new telephone lines.

I am happy to be alive to tell this story to help other people. You never realize what you have until it is gone. If fire is headed your way, don't take it as a joke, thinking, "Oh yeah, I guess I should get my stuff out."

DANNY COLLAZO
PALM COAST, FL

The Story—Part 4

Discovery File

What's Really Burning?

When a candle burns, you probably assume, like most people, that the wick is burning. Surprise! It's not!

As you bring the match toward the candle to light it, the heat from the match causes some of the wax to melt. Now in a liquid form, the wax travels up the wick. As the liquid wax gets near the top of the wick, it's closer to the flame and becomes hotter. When liquids become hotter they *vaporize*, or turn into a gas. That's what happens to the liquid wax, and the vapors of this gas burn in the flame. (The wick itself does burn, but only when the candle burns down to a point that leaves the top of the wick so high in the flame that it can dry out and burn.)

As you may know, atoms in everything around us are vibrating—even the atoms in this piece of paper. At room temperature they are vibrating slowly, but they are still vibrating. The only time atoms don't vibrate is at *absolute zero*, but that's another story.

When matter is heated, its atoms vibrate faster. When the candle is in solid form, the atoms are clumped together and vibrate very slowly. As the wax melts from the heat of the match—and then the heat of the burning wick—the atoms vibrate more quickly. When the candle wax changes into a gas, the atoms are vibrating so much that they move farther apart.

In all fires, it is gases that are actually burning. In fact, when a forest fire rages out of control, the heat of the fire is actually vaporizing the solid materials in its path. The fuel ahead of the fire becomes preheated from the heat of the fire already burning, so its gases ignite even faster.

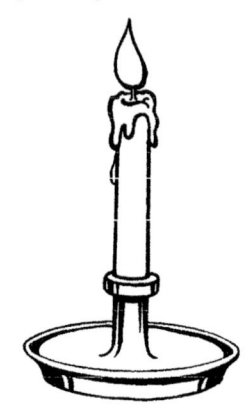

You can try another experiment with a burning candle to find out what happens during combustion. If you place a piece of aluminum foil over the flame for a while, what do you see on the foil?

If carbon, in the form of *soot*, collects on the foil, this indicates that not all of the carbon in the fuel has combined with oxygen to form carbon dioxide. Soot formation is not yet completely understood by scientists. We do know that only certain fuels produce soot.

Candle wax is a hydrocarbon—made primarily of carbon and hydrogen. As it burns, the carbon and the hydrogen each combine with oxygen and are released as carbon dioxide and water. In fact, if you turn a glass beaker upside down over the burning candle, you will see droplets of water collect on the inside of the glass. (The flame will shortly go out, because you are depriving it of a vital side of the fire triangle: oxygen.)

What happens to the candle as it burns? Although the wax may appear to disappear, the law of conservation of mass tells us that matter does not completely disappear. It may change form, but it does not vanish. If you were able to accurately measure the byproducts of the combustion reaction, they would equal the mass of the candle and oxygen together.

Until people understand the science and chemistry of fire, they naturally assume something disappears when it burns, because all they had left was a pile of ashes. However, the truth is that the rest of the matter literally went up in smoke.

OPTIONAL ACTIVITY

Old Faithful Bounces Back?

Purpose
To use Landsat images to analyze regrowth and recovery after a major forest fire.

Materials
- computer with access to the Web to access a time series of Landsat images of Yellowstone National Park

Background
In the spring of 1988, lightening sparked the first of what we now call the Yellowstone fires. But it wasn't until November—half a year later—that heavy snow smothered the last smoldering ember. From spring through summer and into the fall, thousands of firefighters battled the blazes, and millions of gallons of water and chemicals were dropped on the Yellowstone flames. Before it was over, almost a million acres of the park were burned. Another half-million acres of forest outside the park were also destroyed.

Now that it's been more than a decade since the fires, signs of recovery are clearly visible.

Procedure
On July 27, 1988, the Yellowstone fires threatened to burn Old Faithful Lodge, but the wind shifted and the fire turned south. The grand old lodge was saved, but there was great destruction of forest in the Old Faithful Geyser area. Trees, bushes, and undergrowth of all kinds were destroyed in this, the most popular area of Yellowstone National Park.

The superintendent of the park has just been awarded a grant from the U.S. Forest Service. The money is to be used to study the recovery of forests after a fire. Two sites near Old Faithful Geyser will be selected for the study. Both sites must have been severely burned, and one of them must be recovering rapidly while the other must be recovering slowly.

A team of scientists will study the two sites in detail. The scientists will try to determine what factors contribute to a rapid recovery in one case and a slow recovery in the other. Your job, working together with the rest of your class, is to select the two best sites for the team to study.

For this activity, you will need a computer with access to the Web. The Web address www.eventbasedscience.com will take you to Landsat data that show the Old Faithful area before the fires, soon after the fires, and approximately 11 years after the fires. Your teacher will assign each student in your class one of 36 small areas to evaluate. You will click on your area to see three enlarged views for comparison. The questions your class is trying to answer are these:

- Which of the 36 small areas shows the most recovery?
- Which of the areas shows the least recovery?
- How do we determine recovery rates from the satellite data?

Before you start, explore the images and try to decide how you will rank the various areas. How can you compile and display the class data? How will you select the "winners"?

Conclusion
Tomorrow, the superintendent of Yellowstone National Park needs your answer. Which two areas will the scientists study? Prepare a memo to the superintendent in which you name the two areas you have selected. (You may use the letter and number that identify the areas you have chosen.)

Justify your selection by explaining how the areas meet these requirements:

- The sites were both severely burned.
- One site is recovering.
- The other site is either not recovering at all or is recovering very slowly.

DISCOVERY FILE

Recent Disasters and Near-Disasters

With almost every fire-related disaster, valuable lessons are learned. But sadly, these lessons have a cost—they are usually accompanied by loss of life and property—and the recommendations for preventing similar disasters in the future are not always heeded.

September 26, 1997 A thick blanket of smog and smoke over parts of Southeast Asia contributed to a plane crash in Sumatra and the collision of two ships nearby on the same day. Forest fires burning in the jungles of Indonesia and Malaysia obscured the skies for weeks over a large region, causing poor visibility. This ecological disaster began when people started burning Indonesian rain forests. A drought added fuel to the fire, and even El Niño played a role by delaying the monsoons.

Grand Forks, North Dakota, April 1997 After the worst blizzard in recent history, ice in the river, and a devastating flood, what else could happen? Fire! Folks in Grand Forks thought the worst of their disasters were over until April 19, when a blaze swept through the city's downtown—destroying buildings that were already partially underwater from the flood. Fire hydrants were covered with water, and fire trucks were useless because downtown streets were flooded. Airplanes dropped fire-retardant chemicals on the buildings, but despite heroic efforts, much of the town burned and was left in ruins. Electrical problems triggered by floodwater probably started the fire.

Fire on Mir, February 23, 1997 Imagine being 240 miles from Earth, in an enclosed capsule, with a fire burning around you. You don't have a fire hydrant or even a reliable source of water. This is what happened to astronauts and cosmonauts aboard the Russian space station Mir in February 1997 when an oxygen generator leaked and caught fire that threw out four-foot-long jets of flame like a blowtorch. Fire extinguishers were bolted in place, so the crew could not get to them.

The fire began when an astronaut was making a batch of oxygen using a candle-type generator. Flames ignited quickly and burned for 14 minutes until the fire was smothered by combustion wastes. The potentially catastrophic fire proved instrumental in establishing a need to find out more about fire behavior in space. Contrary to some expectations, fire burns quite well in weightlessness, though with some surprising differences from fires on Earth. Astronaut Shannon Lucid found that the birthday candles on her cake on Mir burned for almost 45 minutes. Even more unusual, a candle's flame is in the shape of a sphere.

Since the Mir fire, astronauts have been deliberately setting more fires in space. Knowledge about the behavior of those fires will be critical on future space stations or on a trip to Mars.

Crash of TWA Flight 800, July 17, 1996 Although no one has conclusively proven what caused the tragic explosion and fire that killed all 230 passengers, one theory suggests that faulty wiring may have started it. A report one year after the crash suspects the bundling of high- and low-voltage wiring as the source of sparks, which may have ignited jet-fuel vapors in the central fuel tank. Witnesses on the ground saw streaks of light, which investigators now believe was fiery jet fuel trailing from the belly of the plane. Since the fatal crash, the National Transportation Safety Board (NTSB) has recommended changing the wiring near the central fuel tank.

ValuJet Crash, May 11, 1996 Oxygen canisters played a role in the crash of ValuJet Flight 592. Although the crash was blamed on human error, the real cause was the oxygen in the generators mislabeled and incorrectly stored in the cargo hold. Despite recommendations from the NTSB, airlines have not installed smoke detectors in cargo holds or changed the storage procedures.

Storm King Mountain, July 1994 Fourteen firefighters died in the deadliest U.S. wildfire in recent decades. The wind-whipped fire destroyed many acres in the mountains of Colorado, but not before a team of expert smoke jumpers died. Their deaths were blamed on poor communication and problems with safety procedures at the scene. Among the smoke jumpers who died was 24-year-old Kathi Beck, a member of the Oregon Army National Guard and an elite group of U.S. Forest Service firefighters known as the *Hot Shots*. Since this tragedy, the makers of fire shelters—a last resort for firefighters in wildfires—have improved them. But the best fire shelter made cannot protect firefighters from a fire traveling 100 feet per minute.

Oakland, California, fire, October 1991 Fire season in California is notoriously treacherous, especially when the Santa Ana winds come in the fall. In 1991, fires in Oakland and Berkeley claimed 25 lives, destroyed more than 3000 residences, and caused an estimated $1.5 billion in property damage.

High winds and dense vegetation help fires spread rapidly, so homeowners are advised to cut down flammable brush around their homes to create a fire-safe zone. But despite repeated warnings, people continue to move into these dry areas, where fire is inevitable. And many ignore the steps that could save their homes.

IN THE NEWS

Why wait for redesign to lessen fuel-tank dangers?

In the 17 months since TWA Flight 800 exploded over the Atlantic Ocean, a reluctant consensus has formed: The fuel tanks on commercial jets may be far more dangerous than was previously assumed.

In Baltimore Tuesday, Boeing joined the consensus.

A company official said fuel vapors pose enough of a danger to warrant consideration of jetliner design changes. Not just in 747s like Flight 800 but in all jets.

That acknowledgment, during National Transportation Safety Board (NTSB) hearings into the crash, comes six days after the Federal Aviation Administration (FAA) similarly reversed its previous opinion.

For four decades, plane manufacturers and the FAA, which regulates them, had insisted that the flammability risk of fuel fumes, known to build up in empty tanks, was minimal as long no spark was present to ignite them. Jetliners were designed accordingly, assuming that if all ignition sources were eliminated, safety was assured. Yet TWA 800's fuel tank, like that on a 737 seven years ago in the Philippines, exploded for still unexplained reasons.

A re-evaluation, urged by the NTSB for a year, clearly is overdue. But executing the design changes and retrofitting planes could take years.

In the meantime, efforts to minimize risk are moving at a crawl. A year ago, after five months of investigating Flight 800's fuel-tank explosion, the NTSB recommended several precautions. Some were long-range and costly, and the FAA understandably did not rush to mandate them.

But the NTSB also suggested faster, cheaper methods. Operational changes such as:

▶ Carrying more fuel in the center wing tanks, which often fly near empty to conserve flight time and money.
▶ Refueling tanks before takeoff with fuel from cooler ground tanks.
▶ Adding information to crews' flight handbooks about fuel-tank temperatures.

The FAA and the industry disputed the merits of these interim steps, just as they disputed the NTSB's assertions that the fuel tanks posed a risk. Now that they've rethought the need for addressing fuel vapor dangers, a rethinking of interim steps seems critical.

Redesign in the works
The explosion of TWA Flight 800's center fuel tank may now lead to the redesign of all jets:

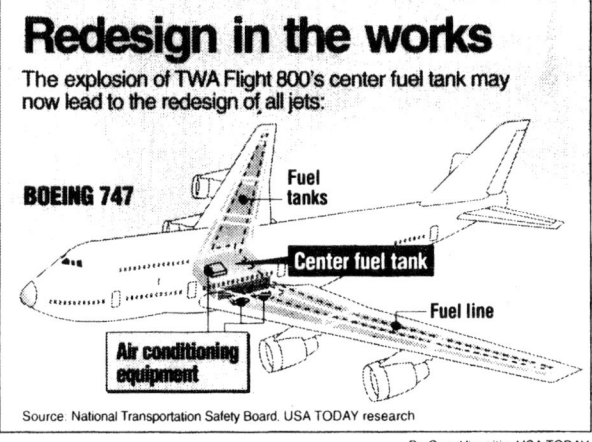

BOEING 747 — Fuel tanks, Center fuel tank, Fuel line, Air conditioning equipment

Source: National Transportation Safety Board, USA TODAY research
By Gary Visgaitis, USA TODAY

USA TODAY, 11 DECEMBER 1997

IN THE NEWS

On the mountain, 14 grim reminders

The 14 granite crosses on Storm King Mountain are 2 feet high, with a 1-foot cross-arm. They are secured in the ground to a depth of 3 feet with concrete.

"We wanted them to be permanent," says Bob Mackey, whose son Don was among the casualties.

The most difficult crosses to place belong to firefighters Richard Tyler and Robert Browning. When the South Canyon Fire blew up, they died in a steep, rocky chute.

Family members of the dead have returned to the fire scene, and many of the crosses are decorated. Alongside her cross, to honor her Indian heritage, Terri Hagen's memorial includes a circular sculpture with pieces of metal that resemble feathers. When the wind blows, the metal sounds like chimes.

Other remembrances include a homemade sign that reads, "Gone But Not Forgotten."

At dusk on July 6, the community of Glenwood Springs, Colo., will dedicate a memorial to the 14 who lost their lives.

— *Tim Wendel*

USA TODAY, 14 JUNE 1995

The Story—Part 4   65

INTERDISCIPLINARY ACTIVITY

Social Studies: Calamity Laws

Purpose
To write a newspaper article about the history of fire safety laws in the United States.

Background
In my town, it's hard to get our local government to take action. We petitioned the city council to add a traffic light at a busy intersection, but nothing happened. If action is ever taken, it won't be petitioning that convinces our leaders. A traffic light will never be installed unless a fatal accident happens!

No matter how logical it might seem to spend money on safety, local governments everywhere often wait until tragedy forces them to act. Procrastination on safety isn't new, either; there are many examples of it from our history. For instance, where did modern fire safety laws come from?

Materials
- The Story, Parts 3 and 4 (see pages 30, 31, 47, and 48)

Procedure
National Fire Prevention Week can be either the first or second week of October, but it always contains October 9—the anniversary of the Great Chicago Fire. You are a social scientist who is an expert on how the world has changed and how it might change in the future. You have been hired by the local newspaper to work together with two or three of your colleagues to write an article for their Fire Prevention Week edition of the paper. They want you to use your knowledge of history to explain where our modern fire safety laws came from.

Together with your partners, read and discuss Parts 3 and 4 of the Story. Select three or four famous fires, and discuss how each fire led to new laws about fire safety or prevention. Focus your discussion on the relationship between the cause of a fire, or deaths from the fire, and the type of law that was passed.

Conclusion
Now write a draft of the article—but before you begin, decide who will do what. Your team is responsible for the entire article, but each of you is responsible for writing about only one of the fires. Divide the job so that the final article is as good as it can be.

Work with your team to add a catchy headline, a strong introduction, and a conclusion to your article.

Interdisciplinary Activity

Math: Warm-up Activities

Purpose
To practice math skills using the context of fires.

Procedure
Do these warm-up activities as directed by your teacher.

1. Determine the weight of material you need to make 16 fire-retardant uniforms for your local fire department. The fire-retardant material weighs 7.5 ounces per square yard, and you will need 2.5 square yards to make one uniform.
2. Ms. Chang has been asked to report the percentage of days that the cabins in Camp Muddy Knee will be used. If cabins are needed on four of every seven days, determine the percentage use for the cabins.
3. In many parts of the world, land area is measured in *hectares*. In the United States we use acres. One hectare is equivalent to about 2.47 acres. Which forest had the most devastation from its recent forest fire: a forest in California that lost 10,251 acres, or a forest in Quebec in which 7334 hectares were destroyed?
4. Before the fire, the diameter of the campfire ring at Camp Muddy Knee was 30 feet. What was the area inside the old ring? How much larger will the area of the new campfire ring be if the diameter is increased by 4 feet?
5. In the summer of 1970, a fire at Camp Horsefly destroyed 24 acres of forest. In the years since the fire, 8 acres have grown back as meadowland, 4 acres are now used for a vegetable garden, and the rest have been replanted in forest. What is the ratio of open land to forest in this area? Express your ratio as a fraction in simplest terms.
6. In Canada, the following data were recorded for July 8, 1997:

Province or Location	Area Burned (hectares)
British Columbia	8
Quebec	3
Yukon Territory	6
Newfoundland	0
Alberta	29
New Brunswick	2
Northwest Territory	0
Nova Scotia	2
Saskatchewan	6
Prince Edward Island	0
Manitoba	13
National Parks	1
Ontario	2

   a. Make a stem-and-leaf plot of the data.
   b. Find the mean number of hectares burned on that day. Also find the median and the mode of the data.
   c. Explain which measure of central tendency—mean, median, or mode—best describes the data.
   d. Find the lower quartile and the upper quartile, and make a box-and-whisker plot of the data.
   e. Tell which plot—the stem-and-leaf plot or the box-and-whisker plot— you think gives a better visual picture of the data, and explain why.
7. Of the approximately 125,000 forest fires that occur annually in the United States, 92% result from human causes. Calculate the number of fires resulting from natural causes.

INTERDISCIPLINARY ACTIVITY

Math: Slow Down Those Fire Trucks

Purpose
To calculate travel times between two points using alternate routes.

Background
Speeding on neighborhood streets has been a problem in cities and suburbs of the United States since the invention of the automobile. It used to be that speeders were kept in check by fear and shame—the fear of the police and the shame of being seen by neighbors.

Fear and shame may still be there, but communities across the country are adding what they call "traffic calming" devices to slow the speeders. One of the most popular of these "calming" contraptions is the speed bump—a mound of asphalt that forces cars to slow to 15 miles per hour or less or causes the driver to suffer a bone-jarring jolt.

Procedure
You are a mathematician who lives in a town that is considering the use of speed bumps. Most people object; they claim that speed bumps won't just slow speeders—they will slow fire trucks and ambulances too. Speed bumps, they say, may risk more lives than they protect! Besides, speeders will still speed between bumps.

The mayor has hired you to study the issue. Your job is to calculate the time that will be lost by responding fire trucks if bumps are installed and make a recommendation about whether to go ahead with the bumps.

You plan to first calculate how much extra time it will take for an emergency vehicle to respond if the bumps are installed. Then you will investigate whether the extra time will make a difference.

According to research done by fire officials in Portland, Oregon, each bump adds approximately 10 seconds to emergency-response time. You have determined that it takes 10 seconds for a fire engine to cover one city block, and that a turn adds 5 seconds to travel time. So, without speed bumps, it takes about 60 seconds for a fire engine to drive from the Elm Street Fire Station to the house at 5900 Dog Avenue.

Estimate how long the same trip will take after the proposed bumps are installed. Calculate several different routes, and

Proposed Speed-Bump Placement

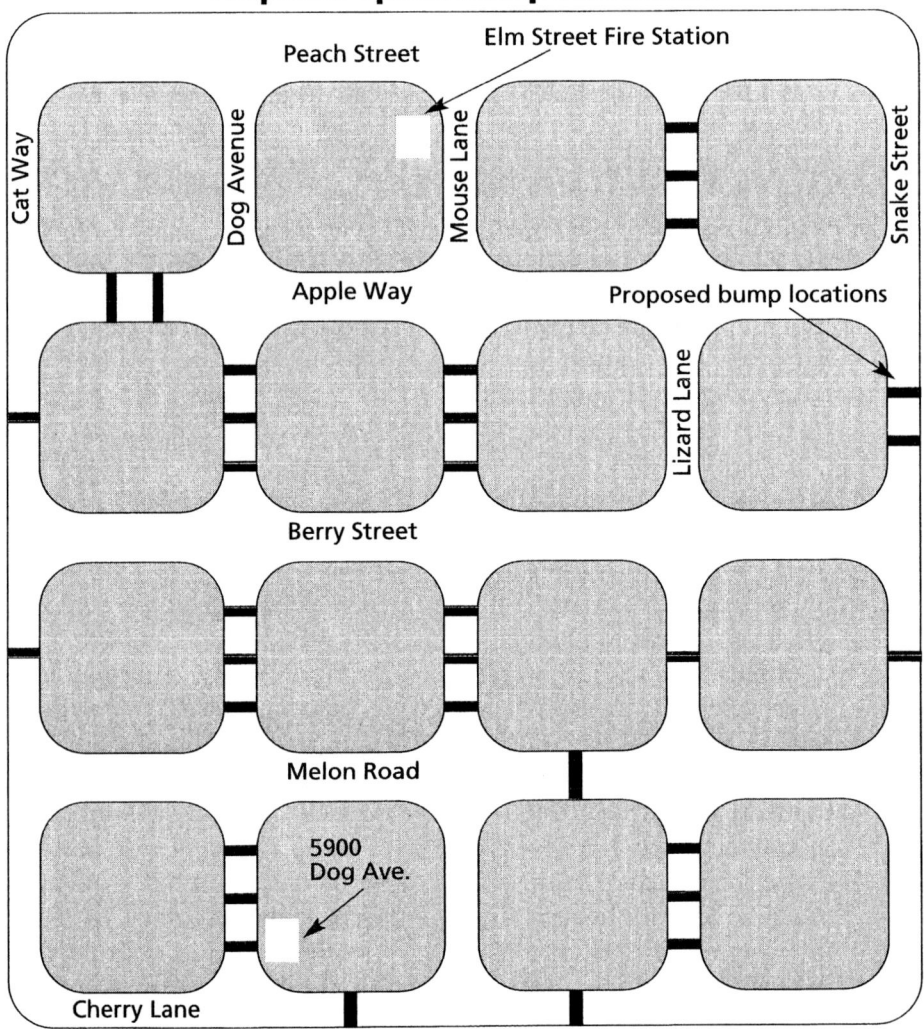

68   Fire!

determine the route that gives the best possible response time.

Note: The Fire Safety Engineering Group at the University of Greenwich in England has published results of tests that indicate it takes only about 3 minutes 40 seconds for a wastebasket fire in a small room to spread to everything in the room. The point at which the room explodes into flames is known as *flashover.*

Conclusion

Write a paragraph with your recommendation for the mayor. Begin your recommendation with these words:

"The city _____ (should or should not) go ahead with the proposed placement of speed bumps on city streets."

Follow this introduction with sentences that give the three strongest reasons for your recommendation. Be sure to mention emergency-response time without speed bumps as compared with the best emergency-response time with speed bumps. Compare the time difference with the speed with which a fire can reach flashover.

Interdisciplinary Activities

Interdisciplinary Activity

English: Descriptive Writing

Purpose
To write a piece of descriptive prose or poetry using personification, metaphor, and sensory images of fire.

Background
From your study of fire, as well as from your own experiences and reading, you know that fire has both positive and negative effects. In myths from various cultures, fire is kept by the gods until someone steals it to bring warmth and the energy for cooking to the people of Earth. Prometheus, the thief of the Greek myth, warns people that fire is greedy and must be watched carefully, for it can be destructive as well as helpful.

Fire evokes strong emotional responses—both positive and negative, just like the outcomes of fire itself. For example, in her poem "Upon the Burning of Our House July 10th, 1666," Anne Bradstreet wrote of the sorrow, fear, and distress she felt as she watched her home burn:

*In silent night when rest I took
For sorrow near I did not look
I wakened was with thund'ring noise
And piteous shrieks of dreadful voice.
That fearful sound of "Fire!" and "Fire!"
Let no man know is my desire.
I, starting up, the light did spy,
And to my God my heart did cry
To strengthen me in my distress
And not to leave me succorless.
Then, coming out, beheld a space
The flame consume my dwelling place.*

In contrast, Sara Teasdale wrote the following lines in "Barter," a poem expressing her awe of fire as one of Nature's most beautiful elements:

*Life has loveliness to sell,
All beautiful and splendid things,
Blue waves whitened on a cliff,
Soaring fire that sways and sings,
And children's faces looking up
Holding wonder like a cup.*

As in Teasdale's poem, fire is often represented as a living thing (it "sings"). This is called *personification*—the assignment of human characteristics to nonhuman entities. You may have heard of fire "racing" as it spreads, or of "tongues of fire," or of flames that "lick" at the logs they burn. In fact, fire-department personnel use the term *head* to label the front of a moving ground fire and "fingers" to indicate paths farther behind the head and progressing outward.

Metaphors (implied comparisons) using the word *fire* or qualities of fire to describe other things are commonplace. Someone may have "fiery" red hair or "fire in her eyes." Another may look "ashen" or have a "blazing" temper. You may be "burning" to do something, or your passion may be "smoldering."

Action verbs are used by writers to create sensory images of fire's characteristics. Fire can roar, crackle, or hiss. It can scorch or merely singe. Its smoke can waft or choke. It can crisp or char your food. Its brilliant yellow flames can leap; its red embers can die.

Procedure
Write a poem or piece of prose (writing using ordinary language) that describes fire or that uses fire as a metaphor for something else. Although you may write about fire in general, your writing may be more effective if you choose a particular fire, perhaps a campfire or bonfire (using positive images) or a house fire or explosion (with negative images).

There are words in the background section (above) that personify fire; that compare fire to other things; and that provide sensory images to help a reader see, hear, feel, smell, and taste fire. You may use some of these words, but also think of original ways to describe fire. You may find the thesaurus a helpful tool to uncover additional nouns, adjectives, and verbs.

After you write a first draft, read your piece to a partner. Ask your partner to comment upon the sense and effectiveness of your writing. Be sure you meet the objective of this activity, which is to use personification, metaphors, and sensory images. If you are writing poetry, listen carefully for the use of rhyme and rhythm. Revise your work until you are satisfied that your piece has the most effective descriptions it can have. Finally, edit your piece so that errors do not distract the reader from your intended response.

PERFORMANCE ASSESSMENT
Writing to Persuade: A Burning Issue

Purpose
To demonstrate knowledge of the nature of fire and the role of fire in nature in a letter to the editor of a local newspaper.

Background
Congratulations! You are the superintendent of a large new state park. As superintendent, one of your jobs is to make sure the plants and animals in the park are healthy. But fire season is coming! The park and everything in it are in danger.

You know that fires play a natural role in the health of a forest. That role can be either positive or negative. Timing is everything.

You have noticed that the forest in your new park is cluttered with dead, dry underbrush and debris—fuel is everywhere. Not only that, but since last spring, there hasn't been any rain. Things are getting drier by the day!

It will be only about two months before things will be so dry that the kindling point will drop to a level that makes a wildfire almost inevitable. And there is no rain in the forecast.

A fire today could be a good thing. A fire in two months will be a disaster.

Procedure
You have decided that what's needed is a controlled burn. To let the public know what you are planning and why you are planning it, you decide to write a letter to the editor of the local newspaper. In your letter, you will try to convince your neighbors that a fire today is the right thing to do. Tell them that it will be under control at all times and that it will make the park safer and healthier in the future.

Begin your letter with an attention-grabbing introduction. Next, tell your readers what fire is and how all three of its components are needed for a fire to burn. Emphasize how the components necessary for a fire are present in the park. Explain what the risk of a forest is today and why it will be greater tomorrow if nothing is done now. Describe the role fire plays in the natural health of a forest. Use facts and data from the science activities and other information in this module to support your statements.

Finally, write a brief conclusion that sums up your points and tells the readers whom to call if they have questions or concerns.

Remember that an exceptional letter
- Has an attention-getting introduction.
- Clearly states an opinion.
- Gives facts to support opinions.
- Has a strong conclusion.
- Is relatively error-free and follows the conventions of grammar.

Use the Proofreading Guidesheet on page 72 to edit your letter. Have your peers evaluate and react to your letter using a copy of the Peer-Response Form on page 73.

Questions
1. How do you get your readers' attention?
2. How and where is your opinion stated?
3. What information about the nature of fire and the role of fire in nature do you include? What other information might you include?
4. What data and facts do you use to support your opinion?
5. What other data might you use?
6. How could you improve your conclusion to make it stronger?

Proofreading Guidesheet

1. Have you identified the assigned purpose of the writing assignment? Have you accomplished this purpose?

2. Have you written on the assigned topic?

3. Have you identified the assigned form your writing should take? Have you written accordingly?

4. Have you addressed the assigned audience in your writing?

5. Have you used sentences of different lengths and types to make your writing effective?

6. Have you chosen language carefully so the reader understands what you mean?

7. Have you done the following to make your writing clear for someone else to read?

    - used appropriate capitalization
    - kept pronouns clear
    - kept verb tense consistent
    - used correct spelling
    - used correct punctuation
    - used complete sentences
    - made all subjects and verbs agree
    - organized your ideas into logical paragraphs

Peer-Response Form

Directions

1. Ask your partners to listen carefully as you read your rough draft aloud.

2. Ask your partners to help you improve your writing by telling you their answers to the questions below.

3. On a sheet of lined paper, jot down notes about what your partners say when you ask these questions:

    a. What did you like best about my rough draft?

    b. What did you have the hardest time understanding about my rough draft?

    c. What can you suggest that I do to improve my rough draft?

4. Ask your partner to use a pencil to place a check mark near any mechanical, spelling, or grammatical construction about which you are uncertain.

5. Return the papers and check your own. Ask your partner for clarification if you do not understand or agree with the comments on your paper. Jot down notes you want to remember when writing your revision.

SCIENCE SAFETY RULES

General
Follow all instructions. Never perform activities without the approval and supervision of your teacher. Do not engage in horseplay. Never eat or drink in the laboratory. Keep work areas clean and uncluttered.

Dress Code
Wear safety goggles whenever you work with chemicals, glassware, heat sources such as burners, or any substance that might get into your eyes. If you wear contact lenses, notify your teacher.

Wear a lab apron or coat whenever you work with corrosive chemicals or substances that can stain. Wear disposable plastic gloves when working with organisms and harmful chemicals. Tie back long hair. Remove or tie back any article of clothing or jewelry that can hang down and touch chemicals, flames, or equipment. Roll up long sleeves. Never wear open shoes or sandals.

First Aid
Report all accidents, injuries, or fires to your teacher, no matter how minor. Be aware of the location of the first-aid kit, emergency equipment such as the fire extinguisher and fire blanket, and the nearest telephone. Know whom to contact in an emergency.

Heating and Fire Safety
Keep all combustible materials away from flames. When heating a substance in a test tube, make sure that the mouth of the tube is not pointed at you or anyone else. Never heat a liquid in a closed container. Use an oven mitt to pick up a container that has been heated.

Using Chemicals Safely
Never put your face near the mouth of a container that holds chemicals. Never touch, taste, or smell a chemical unless your teacher tells you to.

Use only those chemicals needed in the activity. Keep all containers closed when chemicals are not being used. Pour all chemicals over the sink or a container, not over your work surface. Dispose of excess chemicals as instructed by your teacher.

Be extra careful when working with acids or bases. When mixing an acid and water, always pour the water into the container first and then add the acid to the water. Never pour water into an acid. Wash chemical spills and splashes immediately with plenty of water.

Using Glassware Safely
If glassware is broken or chipped, notify your teacher immediately. Never handle broken or chipped glass with your bare hands.

Never force glass tubing or thermometers into a rubber stopper or rubber tubing. Have your teacher insert the glass tubing or thermometer if required for an activity.

Using Sharp Instruments
Handle sharp instruments with extreme care. Never cut material toward you; cut away from you.

Animal and Plant Safety
Never perform experiments that cause pain, discomfort, or harm to animals. Only handle animals if absolutely necessary. If you know that you are allergic to certain plants, molds, or animals, tell your teacher before doing an activity in which these are used. Wash your hands thoroughly after any activity involving animals, plants, plant parts, or soil.

During field work, wear long pants, long sleeves, socks, and closed shoes. Avoid poisonous plants and fungi as well as plants with thorns.

End-of-Experiment Rules
Unplug all electrical equipment. Clean up your work area. Dispose of waste materials as instructed by your teacher. Wash your hands after every experiment.